CAUGHT CARING:

A Model for Serving Others

Pete,

Thank you for endorsing my book.
You helped me with my Christian
walk, encouraged me to read the
Bible, and prayed for Velma and I.
I value our friendship and hope you
enjoy reading the book!
You have always been Caught Caring.

Don
5/27/19

Dr. J. Don Trotter

ISBN 978-1-64140-636-9 (paperback)
ISBN 978-1-64140-638-3 (hardcover)
ISBN 978-1-64140-637-6 (digital)

Christian Faith Publishing, Inc.
832 Park Avenue
Meadville, PA 16335
www.christianfaithpublishing.com

Printed in the United States of America

"I am a Marine Veteran of the Korean war and whole heartily confirm and endorse Caught Caring: A Model for Serving Others. Don recounts how we met, became close friends and shared some of God's miracles in my life. Don and his wife helped when my wife was sick, checked on us each day, prayed for us and encouraged me after the loss of my wife. He drove me to my appointments at the VA and shared meals with me. He even took my dog, Hammer to the vet. We frequently went out for coffee and shared our spiritual journey. Don made my time in Glendale, AZ a better and easier time for me. I also know that Don was giving this kind of time and care to others as well! We can all learn from his model for serving others."

Chaplin Freeman L. Nickel
Seattle, WA

##

"I've known Don since the 1970s when he was a parishioner in my church. I highly recommend Caught Caring: A Model for Serving Others which includes personal stories and a care ministry model that will encourage you to serve others."

Rev. D. J. Burrell
Executive Treasurer and Investment Consultant,
District Development Director and District Stewardship Director
for Peninsular Florida District Council of the Assemblies of God, Inc.

##

"In this much-needed book, Don shares his experiential insight into how to have a productive Care Ministry. He has brought to the forefront the importance of a well-functioning care ministry, and the substantial asset it is to the Body of Christ. The support, comfort and hope it gives to those facing life's many challenges is beyond measure. We are blessed to know Don and his wife Velma. Their love for the Lord and their compassion for others is evident in all they do."

Rev. Manny and Rev. Jean Vieira
Broken Arrow, OK

##

Endorsements

"Structure is often needed to transform good intentions into action. Caught Caring: A Model for Serving Others offers practical steps to help faith communities become a symphony of caring. I am grateful to J. Don Trotter for developing this inspiring book that will do so much to improve life for others."

Elizabeth Banta, M.C.
Executive Director
Duet: Partners in Health & Aging

##

"Dr. Trotter shares his lived experience and allows us to learn how to constructively move forward in work, life and love. This is a wonderful read for those who wish to increase effectiveness and meaning in everyday life."

Cheryl A. Boglarsky, Ph.D.
Director of Research and Product Development
Human Synergistics, Inc.

##

"What a joy to have known Don and Velma since they were teenagers and witnessed their ever-deepening commitment to Christ and His church. They kept us informed of their lives, which took them to different areas of this and other nations and we've seen how their consistent Christian lives have influenced others all along the way. Caught Caring: A Model for Serving Others is a well thought out and organized pattern for serving others, and Don's 'down home' way of storytelling will keep you reading to the end and help you become a more effective servant of Christ."

Rev. Wilbur W. Coates
North Fort Myers, FL

##

"After more than 40 years leading and studying effective disciple-making congregations, two things stand out as pillars of learning. First, in any congregation the most effective evangelist is always the congregation itself, i.e., the quality of their life together which either draws people to Christ or, in some, tragically, turns people away from Christ. Secondly, nothing contributes more directly to quality in congregational life than an effective care ministry. Don and Velma Trotter are two of the most creative, caring, Christ-centered people I have been privileged to know. Their learning about caring ministries within the church is not garnered from books, but in the living laboratory of several congregations which God led them to serve within. Ours was one. I heartily and without reservation recommend their shared learning in Caught Caring: A Model for Serving Others."

Rev. Dr. Roger K. Swanson
Former Director of Evangelism Ministries,
General Board of Discipleship, United Methodist Church
and co-author of *The Faith-Sharing Congregation*

##

"There is nothing more meaningful or satisfying than caring for others. Giving back is as innate as sleep or hunger. CAUGHT CARING is a very practical and professional model of how you can design and implement a care ministry team to serve others."

Dr. Jagdish N. Sheth
Charles Kellstadt Professor of Business, Emory University
Author of *The Accidental Scholar*

Contents

PREFACE

It is a privilege to share personal experiences in volunteering and assisting others through care ministry. The developed and implemented care ministry model will work for any size church or organization. Serving will enrich your lives both personally and spiritually.

The first section of the book highlights the importance of volunteering and the benefits received. The next section focuses on a series of short personal stories where people were caught caring and emphasizes how giving to others is a natural outflow of the love and grace from God to us. In 1 Peter 4:10 (NIV), we read, "Each one should use whatever gift he has received to serve others, faithfully administering God's grace in its various forms."

Section 3 relates to change, leadership, teamwork, and encouragement when moving forward in a new direction on a project, initiative, or committee. This is followed by featuring a proven care ministry model, thoughtfully developed and implemented with positive results. In the last chapter, the reader is given an opportunity to create, design, and implement their own care ministry team model.

ACKNOWLEDGMENTS

I would like to thank my wife, Velma, for her support, input, encouragement, and assistance. The Lord has given many blessings to me and my family.

In addition, a special thank you for two of my friends, Dot La Motta and Sharon Mankins. Dot is an experienced proofreader and has helped me through editing various stages of the book. Sharon Mankins is a professional artist and provided the beautiful art designs for the book cover and other drawings.

INTRODUCTION

On a warm July morning, I had a few minutes to reflect about how I would mentally work through the fog of a diagnosis and future treatments planned for my wife. Her oncologist discussed with us how chemo was necessary to complete the fight against non-Hodgkin's lymphoma. From recent scans, it was clear the fifteen radiation treatments had made good progress. It was hard not to struggle as I listed in my mind the known side effects we had heard from her doctor.

The nurse called for my wife to come to a room for blood tests. The results would let the doctor know if he should proceed with his schedule for a treatment that day. She was in the normal range, and a chemo cocktail was mixed and infusions began. I took a glance around the room and saw people in other chairs who were all ages, genders and nationalities, some sleeping, others reading books and newspapers.

Memories started rushing in, and I thought back many years when we first met as teenagers. She was the registrar for a conference-wide youth retreat, and her long brown hair, green eyes, and smile were eye-catching. The attendees filed past the table, inquiring about meals and scheduled activities, but I only had one question: did she have a boyfriend?

As an only child, my parents were supportive of my activities outside of school. My dad was gifted with mechanical and electrical skills, which he willingly shared with our neighbors and friends. His job required long hours, but his free time was when he enjoyed tackling anything in need of fixing.

The time came when my junior high friends invited me to a church with an active youth group. I wanted to go. Some Sunday mornings, a church member would pick me up, and occasionally my mother drove and would stay for services. I started volunteering for mission projects along with my friends.

This retreat was an opportunity to meet other Christian youth from across the entire state. The agenda included Bible classes, fellowship, and games of baseball and football. The weekend was fun, and I knew once I was back home, I had to call Velma to ask if she was available to attend a Youth for Christ meeting. These Saturday night gatherings were designed to include films, Bible teachings, and singing. I dialed her number, not knowing the exact words I would use to ask her for a date. She answered the phone, and, to my disappointment, told me she was in the middle of helping her mother prepare dinner and would call me back. Was this just a brush-off? Obviously not since my phone rang a few minutes later and we talked about the retreat and the coming Saturday night. She quickly let me know she was not allowed to ride in a car for a date until the age of sixteen. She assured me a parent or a sibling would bring her and pick her up after the meeting. She was the youngest of six (three brothers and two sisters), and I soon learned her brothers were protective of their little sister. I was told at the retreat she was fond of another boy, coincidentally also named Don, and the good news was he just moved out of state. The other Don was miles away, and all was looking better.

I wanted my driver's license as soon as I reached my sixteenth birthday. My parents helped me purchase a used English A40 Austin, and my contribution came from earning money cutting and trimming yards and working in a grocery store. If I was going to drive, I had to also split the cost of insurance on this car. The car was needed since I played clarinet in the marching band, attended after school clubs and weekly Boy Scout meetings.

Our "unofficial" dating continued for several months with Youth for Christ and sometimes meeting at a local library. When Velma turned sixteen, we alternated our time for both youth groups with one Sunday night at her church and the next at my church. The two pastors were aware of our situation and understood our uncomplicated plan.

Youth group activities included miniature golf, bowling, high school football games, concerts, and an occasional party. We attended rival high schools, and our time to see each other was limited. After school, we briefly talked on the phone, and, believe it or not, her phone was part of a party line, something totally unheard of today. With six kids in the family, her father needed to limit time for each call. He decided five minutes was enough, and frequently you could hear another party line person pick up and anonymously listen in on your conversation.

In my senior year, I asked Velma to wear my high school ring so everyone could know we were "going steady." I graduated and enrolled in summer classes at the community college. The finances in our family were limited, and the possibility for paying tuition to a four-year university was out of the question. The draft was in force, and I decided to fulfill my military obligation, which was a smart choice. I enlisted in the US Army, and military life began with basic training in South Carolina. Velma's last year of high school included a full load of classes, student council, acapella choir, and daily morning readings from the Old Testament over the school-wide intercom.

When Velma was close to graduating, I was home on a short furlough. We talked about a wedding date, and Velma agreed but also let me know there was a catch. A family tradition was prospective husbands were required to ask permission for a daughter's hand from her dad. This was slightly scary but knew it had to be done, so we set a time to meet. Her dad, a dairy farmer, was well known in the community as the go-to guy when other farmers needed to borrow equipment or were short on manpower. He could be described as a no-nonsense guy but with a big heart. I nervously asked him the question. He surprised me when he came back with, "You have my permission if you can give my daughter the style of living to which she has become accustomed." This was funny since Velma grew up on a two-hundred-acre dairy farm, and the "style" was modest and frugal living. I assured her dad she would be taken care of but also knew it might be financially difficult on an army corporal's salary.

The wedding was scheduled one year out, and I was assigned to several army training schools before landing at Fort Knox, Kentucky. I was assured this would be somewhat permanent, and Velma began mailing boxes of fresh baked brownies. The army buddies in the barracks looked forward to mail call and new supplies of goodies. During the first six months at Fort Knox, Velma and one of her sisters traveled to Kentucky for a visit. It was fun to show her around, and I managed to set up a double date for her sister with an army friend.

The engagement year was over, and our wedding day arrived. Velma had organized and finished all preparations while I was one thousand miles away. It was a large wedding, and no one was excluded. Her pastor, my pastor, and my granddad, a Methodist pastor, were integral parts in the wedding ceremony, and the three men did a great job of tying a very tight knot. About two hundred friends and relatives attended, and true to how traditional Southern style receptions were hosted at the time, we chose simple but stylish. We went from the ceremony to a local restaurant's banquet room where the front tables were covered with a wedding cake, punch, coffee, nuts, and mints that would be served to this large crowd. Everyone enjoyed a couple of hours of fellowship and an opportunity to congratulate the new couple. After a short honeymoon, we packed our small car and headed for the hills of Kentucky. We were young to be on our own, but the dependence on each other was the best beginning we could have hoped for.

From our early teenage years, we knew volunteering was going to be an important part of our lives. The needs of others had been key to how we were raised and having parents who helped others.

This book, *Caught Caring: A Model for Serving Others*, shares personal stories of individuals who reached out in one way or another to assist someone in need, and we caught them caring. The model that follows all the stories can be useful to encourage others with a passion to help others, and, in turn, they will be caught caring.

CHAPTER 1

The Benefits of Giving:
Why Volunteer?

"The Lord Jesus said, 'It is more blessed to give than to receive'" (Acts 20:35, NIV).

It was late one Monday evening when the phone rang. It was the pastor of our church, and after a few moments of casual conversation, a question was asked: "Would you consider being chair of the care ministry team?"

My immediate unspoken thought was, *Do what?*

I have a close friend who served in the US Marine Corp and received the nickname of "Do What?" It seems every time someone asked him to do something, his reply was, "Do what?" That was exactly the way I felt when this question was posed to me. After all, my background did not include medical training, and there must be someone more qualified than me.

Some people are misinformed when they think volunteering is only for the retired, and it must always be in the area where that person garnered some professional expertise. Volunteering was not a new concept since my parents encouraged me from an early age to give time to help others.

In Joel Osteen's book titled, *Your Best Life Now: 7 Steps to Living at Your Full Potential,* he indicates "one of the greatest challenges we face in our quest to enjoy our best lives now is the temptation to live selfishly." He states, "You will have more joy than you dreamed possible when you live to give." He goes on to say, "Society teaches us to look out for number one, what's in it for me? Referred to as the me generation. No matter how much they acquire for themselves, they are never satisfied. You must learn to be a giver and not a taker."[1]

In another book, *Why Good Things Happen to Good People* by Stephen Post and Jill Neimark, it says, "Giving is the one kind of love you can count on, because you can always choose it: it's always within your power to give."[2]

Mark 10:45 (NIV), reads, "For even the Son of Man did not come to be served, but to serve, and to give His life as a ransom for many."

I began volunteering in elementary school as a patrol boy and continued with Cub Scouts and Boy Scouts. Attending a small church provided opportunities to assist in Sunday school and then performing in an accordion band with an audience of senior citizens. As an adult, volunteering in churches and other nonprofits has been important to me. When the request came from the church's senior pastor to chair care ministry, it was immediately after I had served for three years as chair of another committee.

In the book titled *Giving: How Each of Us Can Change the World*, William Jefferson Clinton states that, "In the United States, about 55 percent of American adults, almost 84 million people, give some time every year."[3] The USA is blessed by generous, caring people who keep the wheels of time turning as their hearts and hands reach out to others.

My strong belief is everyone needs to experience giving and volunteering their time, talent, and treasure. According to some of my research, there are a variety of benefits to the individual who volunteers his/her time to help others.

Laura-Arrillaga-Andreessen in her book titled *Giving 2.0: Transform Your Giving and Our World*, "Being happier as a result of giving will increase your productivity at work, enrich your relationships at home, and put your own problems into perspective by focusing on the greater problems of others." She referenced a paper by Stephen G. Post, a renowned bioethicist who cited work conducted by researchers at Brown University medical school. The paper indicated that "people who volunteer tend to have fewer of the symptoms of depression."[4]

Harvey Mackay wrote about something his father shared with him that made his life much better. Mr. Mackay wrote in his article titled "Volunteer Your Way to Success" that his father's advice to volunteer was some of the best he had ever received. "He told me I would never have any trouble finding opportunities. And he told me that between 20 and 25 percent of my time should be devoted to this pursuit." Reprinted with permission from Nationally Syndicated columnist Harvey Mackay, author of the New York Times #1 bestseller "Swim with the Sharks Without Being Eaten Alive."

Harvey also stated, "People who do volunteer work and help others on a regular basis have a healthier outlook on life. They are inclined to be go-getters, and consistently report being happier and more contented . . . It doesn't matter whether you are young or old, a student or a professional, working your way up or at the top of your game. Needs abound wherever you are."[5]

I'm not alone with finding through my years of experience that giving to someone else makes you feel better about yourself and the world around you. It's also been a revelation in discovering it is easier to give than to receive. I will talk more about this later in the book.

According to "The Health Benefits of Volunteering: A Review of Recent Research," national and community service, USA Freedom Corps, older volunteers (age sixty or older) are most likely to receive greater health benefits from volunteering. "Those who volunteer have lower mortality rates, greater functional ability, and lower rates of depression later in life than those who do not volunteer." To support this, the US Census Bureau and the Center for Disease Control find "states with a high volunteer rate have lower rates of mortality and incidences of heart disease."[6]

There is no limit when it comes to age in serving God and serving others. We can recite numerous people who are mature in age and are written about in the Bible (e.g., Noah, Abraham, Moses, Joshua, etc.). Many older adults want to continue to be actively involved in serving others.

Stephen Post and Jill Neimark, in their book titled *Why Good Things Happen to Good People,* referred to Doug Oman of the University of California at Berkeley. Oman referenced a thirty-year study of 427 women in upstate New York. The results indicated that "volunteers not only live longer but are healthier" and "those who did any kind of volunteering had better physical functioning thirty years later."[7]

Quite a few years ago, I found a book, *Try Giving Yourself Away* by David Dunn, that inspired me to continue volunteering and giving to others. The author's focus was to practice giving himself away "with no strings attached" and observed others as a hobby while he traveled on business.[8] This book was powerful, and his ideas remained with me over the years. It was discovered while attending a retreat at a Catholic convent. My wife read the book from the convent library during the retreat and shared the contents with me when we returned home. It has gone through several copyrights since 1947. I've ordered copies to give to family and friends and try practicing some examples by giving myself away.

According to Brad Formsma in his book *I Like Giving,* "When we choose to give, we change, and the people around us change. When we move from awareness to action, miracles happen. When we allow giving to be our idea, a world of possibilities opens up before us, and we discover new levels of joy."[9]

In Luke 6:38 (NIV), it says, "Give, and it will be given to you. A good measure, pressed down, shaken together and running over, will be poured into your lap. For with the measure you use, it will be measured to you."

A perfect example of this in my opinion is when a friend of mine was given the District Award of Merit from the Boy Scouts of America. This award is available to Scouters who render service of an outstanding nature at the district level. They gave it to my friend, at least in part, for volunteering with the Boy Scouts for over sixteen years in numerous positions.

He was invited to attend the Annual District Awards Dinner and was only told that he would receive some type of an award. When he arrived for the dinner, he noticed that his family was there, as well as other Boy Scout leaders and Boy Scouts that he had mentored over the sixteen years.

A favorite quote is from James D. Miles: "You can easily judge the character of a man by how he treats those who can do nothing for him."

After high school graduation, I volunteered to become part of the US Army. It was a time in my life when I was seeking direction and guidance. Very early on the first morning of basic training in Fort Jackson, South Carolina, I was questioning my decision and thought, *What have I done?* It ended up being a maturing and learning experience for four years, and I would not trade the time for anything else. I am happy I could serve my country, and it allowed me the opportunity to mature and gain skills I needed. Later, I accessed the GI Bill and continued my studies through several higher education degrees.

After completing a postgraduate education, I taught marketing at a university for seven years. During that time, I joined the Jaycees and worked tirelessly with a committee to bring a new Washington, DC, project called Reading is Fundamental (RIF) to our local community. RIF is one of our nation's oldest and largest nonprofit children's literacy organization in Washington, DC, and provides books to children who might not otherwise have access to them. Working with this organization and knowing more children had books to read was rewarding to me as a volunteer.

"When we lose one blessing, another is often most unexpectedly given in its place" (C. S. Lewis).

In the next chapter on caring with passion, I have included personal, heartfelt stories of volunteers who were the inspiration and motivation for writing this book.

These personal stories are about friends, family members and others who have been caught caring and have given their time and effort to serving others. I regret I cannot mention everyone I have known who gave love and care to others.

CHAPTER 2

Caring with Passion

Short personal stories about people caught caring.

"For where your treasure is, there your heart will be also" (Matthew 6:21, NIV).

Grandpa Fedder

After teaching college, I received a job offer from a company with headquarters in the Northeast. We were living in the southern part of the United States with many family members nearby. It was my wife and I and our two daughters who trekked off to this "new land." As a family, we discussed the possibility of "adopting" a grandmotherly type person living in an assisted living facility near our home. We wanted our daughters to experience friendship with an older woman who might fill the gap left with their grandparents being many miles away. According to the book titled *Giving 2.0: Transform Your Giving and Our World* by Laura Arrillaga-Andreessen, "Community service as a family is also a way of introducing your children to giving and the idea of caring for others, while also showing them how they can contribute to solving some of your community's problems."[10]

Our plans for a grandmotherly type person didn't quite jell. It turned out we were asked to get to know a gentleman we fondly called Grandpa Fedder. The elderly gentleman and his wife resided in the care facility for five years before the wife passed away. They did not have children, and we discovered he didn't have any living family members. Our home was near the care facility, and we visited him for almost five years before he passed away.

I'd like to share a little about Grandpa Fedder and how he was a blessing to our family. There was a little fear and trepidation at first since he was not very warm and friendly, confined to a wheelchair and refused to wear his teeth. Who was he as a person? He was very private and reluctant to share. We started gathering bits and pieces of information through our visits. His vocation had been building kitchen cabinets out of his home garage. We continued in building trust with him. What did he like to do? He loved to watch baseball, eat chocolate candy, and drink a beer. He only had a few teeth and did not wear his dentures, so eating had to be limited to soft food. I remember several times during visits to his room, he would have a piece of roast beef or hamburger remaining on his plate. I knew he could not chew the meat, and I began walking to the facility's kitchen to politely ask to please bring him a peanut butter sandwich or soup so he could eat for nourishment.

He was not inclined to be a conversationalist but did decide to share a secret code from his calendar hanging on the wall near his bed. Using this code, as he explained it to me, I could determine when the facility gave him a bath and other things that only he and I knew at the time. Because of this, I could talk to the nurse and ask her questions, (e.g., why he had not had a bath that week). The personnel at the facility knew Grandpa Fedder did not talk very much, so I'm sure they wondered how I knew this. I never revealed our secret since it was too much fun being a buddy incognito.

What Grandpa Fedder loved most was receiving mail. I took joy in sending him postcards when I traveled, and my oldest daughter who attended college in Virginia sent him mail on a regular basis. This reminded me of mail call when I served in the US Army away from home.

One of the highlights for the family was having him over to our home and driving him to his former neighborhood for a visit. We drove him to his old home where he lived with his wife for many years. I recall his former next-door neighbor coming out to the car and crying like a baby when she realized who I had in my car. All the stories he communicated to me about his business and family occurred in that house. Grandpa Fedder reminisced through teary eyes and a weak smile as his glance focused on the garage doors. I could almost hear the electric saw cutting a fine piece of wood for a beautiful kitchen cabinet and the hours of painstaking detail to make it perfect for his customers. We learned Grandpa Fedder was a perfectionist, and his cabinets were a professional work of art.

One big reward we received when he passed was a request from the facility to write his obituary. Since he didn't have family who visited, the facility director and others thought I might be distantly related. I had the privilege of attending his funeral and helping to celebrate his life with heartfelt words and many fond memories of a gentleman master carpenter.

We received much more than we could give this gentleman we fondly grew to love as Grandpa Fedder. Shortly after his passing, I was on a business trip in Maryland when someone who looked exactly like him passed by a window where I was sitting. I got up and ran outside but was not able to find him. I think he wanted me to know that he loved me and my family and that he was in a good place. In Hebrews 13:2 (NIV), it says, "Do not forget to entertain strangers, for by so doing some people have entertained angels without knowing it."

> *"There's inspiration at our elbows every day if we just knew each other's story" (Captain Gerald Coffee, US Navy Ret.).*

Angel in Disguise

In childhood, I lived in the South and was fortunate to be given the opportunity to visit my grandparents every summer in another state. My granddad was a minister and regularly pastored several churches at one time. This was a special time in my life to learn about God's love at an early age and observe granddad's ministry to many people of diverse cultures.

I recall a Sunday when my granddad took me to a very small church and, before the service started, whispered to me about a surprise for me at the close of service. I sat patiently and counted the minutes until dismissal and then discovered the congregation always had a picnic each week. The church was filled with local farmers from this small community, and they brought vegetables, meats, and desserts for the picnic. I thought this was my surprise, but I found out a little later it was still ahead. My granddad and I were the guests, so we were ushered to the front of the line to fill our plates with delicious food and a big glass of sweet tea to drink.

After a word of prayer, others in the church began to serve themselves. I watched as parishioners lined up and quickly noticed something unusual. They were not carrying a plate but just a large spoon. The spoons were large tablespoons with handles long enough to reach to the bottom of the deep dishes. As they moved around the tables, if they wanted green beans or cream corn, they would take a spoonful and eat over the table without sitting down. They held the chicken with one hand while they continued to move around the table and serve themselves with more vegetables, and all was well. They would occasionally take a sip of tea as they moved their glass from place to place on the table. When it was time for dessert, the long tablespoons were used as they continued to circle the tables. I remember being happy to have served myself enough the first time around, including dessert, so it was not necessary to get a second helping. It was a different time in our lives when the possibility of passing germs to others was not a consideration in this small country church. They were family, and God had blessed the food.

On another occasion, I attended a service where my granddad was responsible for baptizing two elderly people in a small babbling brook that gently curved around giant oak trees with singing birds and beautiful wildflowers. We were surrounded by God's creations for a momentous occasion. My granddad and the people to be baptized wore regular clothes as they prepared to step into the cold water. The first to be baptized was the gentleman. He hung on to my granddad as they eased their way into the water. Suddenly, the man and my granddad disappeared below the creek's surface. Apparently, there was a large slippery rock in the creek they were standing on, and they both slid off into the deep cold water. All the observers standing on the creek's edge were dumbfounded, including me. We were not sure what we should do when up popped my granddad and the gentleman. My granddad was able to get to higher ground and complete the baptism. Once the gentleman stepped out of the water, I could sense his wife was not anxious to be baptized, but as time would tell, the rest went well.

There are other stories to tell about time spent with my granddad, but I will go forward a few years to when he visited my parents. My grandparents had been married for sixty-five years before my grandmother passed away a few months prior to my granddad's visit. My family lived in another part of the state, and granddad's plans were to travel to our home for a visit. The visit did not happen since granddad had a massive heart attack and was taken to a hospital near where my parents lived. My dad notified his two sisters, and they traveled to his location to help.

While granddad was in the hospital, my parents and aunts relayed to me about a nice male nurse who said his name was Mr. Angel. He seemed to always be around, available to sit and talk with the family. Prior to granddad's passing, my dad told me granddad spoke the words, "I'm ready to go home." The family understood what he meant. A comforting scripture came to mind as they recalled Psalm 34:7 (NIV): "The Angel of the Lord encamps around those who fear him, and he delivers them." After his passing, my dad and aunts wanted to thank Mr. Angel for giving his time to show care and concern. They asked the nurses and others to locate Mr. Angel but were told no one on staff answered by that name or description. Who was this mysterious Mr. Angel?

The memorial service for granddad took place in one of many churches where my granddad had served. I was one of the pallbearers, and this was an honor for me. The service was filled with stories celebrating the life of granddad, and many shared how he had touched them with his friendship, love, trust and comfort through his ministry. In the hearse on the way to the grave site, I heard other pallbearers talking about seeing someone standing behind the stained-glass window at the rear of the church. I shared this story with my aunt and uncle who attend that church, and they told me several other people had made the same comment to them. My aunts went back to the church to check on whether someone may have been working on scaffolding that day since there was no ledge on the two-story-high stained glass window. Is it possible that it was Mr. Angel from the hospital where my granddad had been, or another angel was there on the ledge to celebrate granddad's welcome into heaven? Only granddad knows for sure!

I greatly admire my granddad's life and the time he took to be with me. He was a very gentle man with a full-of-life sense of humor. He always started his sermons with a funny story to get the attention of the congregation and then transition into his message. I remember as a small child asking him if his stories were true. Even though he never directly answered me, he acted like that was one of the funniest things he had ever heard. He enjoyed sharing my question about his stories being true with the entire family while we had dinner that evening. My granddad loved to tell stories during dinnertime. His stories seemed like they would go on forever, and you almost wanted to finish the story for him.

I have thought about my granddad over the years and still think about what I learned from him. At an early age, he gave me a Bible, and on the front page he wrote, "May this be your guide through life," and it was signed "Granddad." I still have that Bible and often think of his God-given wisdom and try to let the Bible be my guide through life.

Mr. Angel, the encourager, and the shadow behind the stained glass window, aided in making our loss easier. Even though both were a mystery and cannot be explained, they were caught caring for our family.

> *"Too often we underestimate the power of a touch, a smile, a kind word, a listening ear, an honest compliment or the smallest act of caring, all of which have the potential to turn a life around"* (Leo Buscaglia).

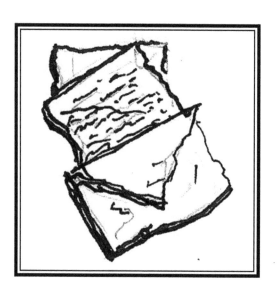

The Lost Letter

My wife was shredding old records one day and came upon a letter from my aunt Alma. In this letter, she talked about a gathering of the Trotter clan in North Carolina, which she described in her letter as a "three ringer." Our daughter was graduating from college, my mother and dad were celebrating their sixtieth wedding anniversary, and our first grandson, who was born just a few months earlier, made his first big public appearance and was welcomed by members of his extended family.

I recall the gathering quite well, and it was very special at the time, but to be reminded of it twenty-one years later from my aunt who is now deceased was extra special. It was a blessing! The gathering began when my parents flew to another state to visit my aunts, Alma and Ouida, with plans to visit family and friends and the church where they were married. After sixty years, the landmarks were not familiar in the town, but the lovely old stone church with beautiful stained glass windows remained constant and unchanged.

About a week after visiting the church, my parents and two aunts drove to my cousin's house in another state to spend the night with her family. They had moved to a small town two years earlier, and this was a first visit for my parents. The next day, they drove three-hours to our meeting place in the college town where our daughter was graduating. We greeted them when they arrived at the hotel where reservations and arrangements were made for all the comforts of home. Some good friends from Florida arrived at almost the same time. These friends had participated in special events for our family over the years, and the gathering would not have been quite right without them. The oldest daughter and family joined the group, and immediately the first grandson (three months old) became the main attraction. Sometime later, our youngest daughter, the one graduating, took time from a busy schedule to greet everyone, and soon thereafter, the cousin and her family arrived.

That evening began as we gathered in a conference room of the hotel to honor my parents for sixty years of marriage. The U-shaped table was decorated with mixed flower arrangements and trays of fresh vegetables and cheese. A delicious dinner was served, and after dinner, I shared words of thanks for the occasion, and the oldest daughter read the "love chapter" from 1 Corinthians 13:1–13. The youngest daughter's boyfriend played the guitar and sang "Above the Clouds," a song he wrote and dedicated to my parents for this celebration. Several attendees spoke of times they shared with my parents, my cousin's family band entertained, and the evening closed with our youngest daughter leading us in prayer.

The next morning, everyone enjoyed a continental breakfast and lunch served in one of the suites. This gave us more time to be together and the younger family members time to get to know one another. The oldest daughter's husband made the weekend exciting for some of our younger members by sharing some hunting experiences and an invitation to go hunting with him. Our future son-in-law played the guitar and taught them a special song.

About 3:00 p.m., our five cars joined a bumper-to-bumper motorcade through the streets of town headed for the big auditorium where graduation exercises would take place. A heavy downpour of rain added to the traffic confusion. The parking lot was several steps from the auditorium and included a steep incline, making it difficult for my mother. A son-in-law was on one side, and I was on the other to pick up my mother and transport her right to a comfortable seat. The graduation speaker was brief but very good. After the ceremony, someone arranged for a delicious barbecue chicken, baked beans, coleslaw, and cake dinner at a local church. To finish the day, we gathered in our room for coffee and to say our goodbyes since we would all go our separate ways the next morning. We were privileged to have my parents accompany my wife and me and our children back to the Northeast. This was such a happy "three ringer" occasion that we vowed to continue our family gatherings in the future. The happy memories we carried away with us are indescribable.

The only way to elaborate on this letter that could have ended up being shredded is that it was a blessing from heaven. Even though we had lived the experiences of the weekend twenty-one years ago, we had let ourselves be caught up in busy times and forgotten good times. I think when my aunt wrote the letter, her focus was to remind us who we are and how God has blessed our family. Copies of the letter were sent to both of our daughters.

We kept our promise to continue our family gatherings by having a reunion with our extended family two years later at a resort near Alma and Ouida's home. For quite a few years after that, we always included my aunt Alma in our immediate family gatherings, such as a tour of Europe, including five countries in nine days, two family reunions in Virginia, and a high-altitude vacation in Winter Park, Colorado. Aunt Alma always exhibited unconditional love for our family, and we look forward to a big reunion in heaven.

When my aunt wrote the letter twenty-one years ago, she did not realize her words would bring joy and happiness again several years after she passed away. She had been caught caring a second time and was a real blessing to others.

Mountaintop Experience

If you've ever been in Arizona in August, you know the blistering summer heat can be quite miserable. We had made plans to leave the desert during the intense temps and headed north in the direction of Winter Park, Colorado. The drive took us through beautiful mountains and towns we had never seen. We arrived in Winter Park early the second day, picked up a key from the rental company, and drove to the large log cabin rented for a family gathering. The cabin was on the outskirts of a national forest, and other homes were barely visible in the distance. You didn't need to think about visiting a gym to run on a treadmill since the outdoors provided opportunities to trek up and down the mountain near the cabin.

My eighty-six-year-old aunt from Tennessee was flying to Denver airport, and we were responsible for picking her up. Other stories in this book mention how the family tried to meet as often as possible at different places for time together.

Our oldest daughter, son-in-law, and three grandsons were driving from South Dakota to join our gathering. The other daughter, son-in-law, and two grandsons were flying from California. It was going to be a coming together to share time and make new memories.

We greeted my aunt at the gate with her small suitcase. She and her husband did not have children, and she was living alone after her husband and sister passed away. She was a career woman, worked in accounting in an auto parts store for many years, and carried her professionalism into her everyday life. She kept up with current events and was an active volunteer in her local church.

Coming back to the cabin, we greeted other family members as they arrived. It was the usual routine to sort out who would be assigned to which bedroom, and we knew the accommodations would give everyone what they needed. The two sets of grandsons were happy to see each other again. They wanted to know what we were going to do and when they could start.

The daughter from California is great with organizing games and projects to keep all grandsons busy. She brought T-shirts and gave instructions for using fabric pens to draw an outline of handprints, writing names of family members in different colors and drawing whatever else they wanted. The shirts were spread out on the porch to dry.

The others were in the kitchen discussing the week's plans for family meals. The previous gatherings always ran along the same line, with each family taking charge of an evening meal to alleviate the same people working in the kitchen all the time. Everyone knew the kitchen was open for breakfast and lunch and you had to make your own meals.

Another established custom was for my wife and the daughters to head off the first day to a local grocery store and bring back food and supplies. The sons-in-law and I were happy to stay behind and put together some sports activities like baseball, football, and even something as simple as walking around the cabin.

With groceries purchased and everyone back in the cabin, we had a relaxing evening and enjoyed the cool mountain air. It was a perfect time to listen to my aunt telling the grandsons some stories about her childhood in Tennessee. We were all tired and got a good night's rest. The next couple of days were filled with exploring the picturesque town and getting ideas for what grandsons might like next. We visited a nearby ski resort and watched as prepared hikers ventured out to climb mountains that in the winter months were easily scaled sitting in a chair lift to reach the top. We saw hikers returning to the bottom looking very exhausted.

The weather was perfect with clear skies, a cool breeze, and bike paths everywhere. My aunt and I had been out in the car and came back to the cabin to discover both daughters, four grandsons, and one son-in-law had rented bikes and were gone. The other son-in-law and his son had driven to visit a friend who lived about fifty miles away. All the family knew they should be back for dinner at 6:00 p.m., and my wife and I had responsibility for cooking that evening.

My aunt helped my wife with preparations of a delicious chicken dish, corn on the cob, corn muffins, salad, an assortment of other vegetables, and, of course, dessert. The table was set, and we expected all remaining family members to come rolling in. The cool mountain air was dropping as the sun began to go behind the mountains. Six o'clock passed, and the son-in-law and grandson who had visited a friend returned and were surprised the rest of the family was not there.

Worry and fear began to creep in as the sun set and still no bicyclists. It was a time when cell phones and cell towers were not as common as they are today. Our son-in-law, grandson, and I tried to think where they might have gone. We were surrounded by a forest. It was now 9:00 pm, so we called the police department to see if there were any reports of accidents in the woods.

Another hour went by, and with officials notified, we prayed for God to be with them and to calm our fear and anxiety. The darkness was one thing, but we knew there were bears roaming the woods. The youngest of the group was a two-year-old grandson.

The son-in-law and grandson, with us, took the car out and drove up and down roads looking for them. My son-in-law is a good hunter and understood the woods better than I did. At eleven o'clock, the cabin phone rang. I grabbed the phone, hoping it was good news, and I was right. The local police had spotted them coming out of the woods and decided it best to take them to the station. I was given instructions to go to the station to identify the group.

Our hearts were filled with praise and gratitude as we piled in the car to go downtown. It was a wonderful reunion, with hugging, kissing, and tears of joy. There was a story to share as we ate our dinner that evening. The group started out on bikes following a trail into the woods. They all were on individual bikes except for a daughter pulling a child trailer with the two youngest grandsons. They were immersed in their enjoyment of the ride, and dusk became darkness while several miles from the cabin. They became concerned and discussed how to go home. Trees were all around, and there was no sun for direction. They admitted they were lost.

They stuck together and just like we were doing in the cabin, prayed to God for help. Several hours later, after trying a couple of different ideas, they saw the lights from the city and came out of the woods where police officers saw them. God was in control for all involved. We were all caught caring, including the police officers, that evening in Winter Park, Colorado.

The remainder of our time together was not so exciting, but we drew closer in realizing how fragile life can be. The son-in-law with the group used this experience as a life lesson and is now a Boy Scout leader.

> *"When I am afraid, I will trust in you. In God, whose word I praise, in God I trust. I will not be afraid" (Psalm 56:3–4, NIV).*

Family Caregivers

I had the opportunity to be a caregiver during the time my wife was going through chemo and radiation. I understand the responsibilities of a caregiver and have known many since serving as a volunteer. As I think back to my childhood, one of the most effective and dedicated caregivers I have ever known was my dad.

My dad was very smart and worked hard on good jobs all his life. My mom also worked for many years but became ill in her early forties and needed care. Her illness was eventually diagnosed as spasmodic torticollis. Before they discovered what was causing her illness, she experienced several experimental surgeries focused on her illness. The MRI machine was not yet perfected and was not commonly used in the 1950s and 60s.

My mother had difficulty keeping her head stationary, and it would involuntarily shake most of the time. The first diagnosis given was reported as a brain tumor. She went through horrific surgery with a hole being drilled in her skull only to be told there was no tumor. The search for a solution was back on again. My dad was always there for my mom and me as a young boy even though he was employed full time. The next surgery was another experiment and required a long-distance trip from Florida to a hospital in New York City. This was a major challenge since I was in junior high and my dad had to be away from his job.

It was seventh grade for me, and I had to learn to manage schedules and school by myself since my dad went with my mom to New York. Being an only child, my dad called to arrange for my meals at a restaurant close enough for me to ride my bike. Thinking back, I'm not sure how my dad was able to handle so much pressure.

A positive point was my dad's career working for a large company with excellent medical insurance. The insurance was a blessing since we didn't have a surplus of money for unexpected expenses such as medical bills. I know God gave him strength to carry on as my mom's caregiver and keep track of me and extra bills. In Philippians 4:13 (NIV), it states, "I can do everything through Him who gives me strength." In Psalm 46:1 (NIV), "God is our refuge and strength, an ever-present help in trouble." These two scriptures helped multiple times to encourage us as we went through trials and tests with my mom's illness.

The trip to New York went well, and she had the experimental surgery and stayed long enough to recover. They were gone a couple of weeks, so I'm sure the Lord was keeping watch over all of us. We did not have family living in our town in Florida, and wonderful neighbors and friends helped keep me on track.

Her condition did not improve this time either, and the doctors decided to do surgery on her neck. Specialists were not available nearby, and another trip to a different state was necessary. Surgery was done on the nerves in her neck, and things went wrong, so almost immediately another operation was required to correct the first surgery.

Mom's pain was not any better after these two surgeries. About the same time, my dad received a letter from his employer giving him notice his medical insurance was being terminated. He had serious worries about the future of his job since he piled up numerous days off to travel for the surgeries. In Isaiah 41:10 (NIV), "So do not fear, for I am with you; do not be dismayed, for I am your God; I will strengthen you and help you; I will uphold you with my righteous right hand."

I look back and recall I might have helped my dad through some of the stresses. He was a quiet man, however, and did not share many of his personal thoughts with me. I was aware, even as a young person, that he must have experienced emotional difficulty in coping, and I was cushioned from the complexities of money issues. Only my parents were knowledgeable of the real story. In retrospect, he must have been experiencing hopelessness when another letter arrived in the mail from his employer. This again proves God has always been in the miracle working business.

The letter stated his large company had been bought out by a much larger one and his medical insurance had been reinstated. It might be easy to write this off as a coincidence and just a matter of good timing, but I would contest that theory. I know this was again God letting us know everything is in His control. My mom continued her search for a medical remedy. Her last surgery was fusing the neck muscles together, and this procedure gave her a status she could adjust and live with. She had to turn her entire body around to look in the direction of someone who was speaking. She still had quite a bit of pain, but the shaking stopped, finally.

My dad continued to be the ultimate caregiver and was there for her every day. I know better now what he must have experienced as a caregiver since I've also been one. It was a privilege to have my dad live with us after my mom passed away.

"The only rock I know that stays steady, the only institution I know that works is the family" (Lee Iacocca).

The Lamb Dinner

I'll share a story of a young man named Earl who was physically and mentally challenged because of abuse from a family member. He was severely disfigured, and it was difficult for him to walk. He lived in a rickety old trailer in a small park and, since he didn't have a car, requested a ride to church.

My wife and I picked him up each Sunday for church services. We developed a relationship, and Earl began to share his sad history. He grew up on a farm, and as a young child, his father was physically abusive with beatings from his belt.

Our family continued getting acquainted with him and invited him to dinner. He wanted to show appreciation for the invitation by purchasing what he could afford to bring. On this occasion, he brought over a package of lamb and wanted to help our family cook and prepare the lamb for dinner.

We had never had an opportunity to eat lamb or prepare it, but my wife cooked it to the best of her ability, and we had it for dinner. It was a good time to experience someone's thank-you for our service. This reminds me now of something I had to later learn: it is easier to give than to receive.

One Christmas, our family gave Earl an electric blanket since we thought he was living in the trailer without heat. When we went to pick him up for church one Sunday morning, we noticed he had been covering up with the blanket but not plugging it in. We reminded him the blanket would operate when plugged in to keep him warm.

Earl seemed to love the Lord and wanted to participate in as many activities as possible at church. He enjoyed being with people and didn't let his challenges hold him back.

Sometime later, I received a job offer and relocated to another city. We tried to keep in touch with Earl but finally lost contact with him. A few years later, someone told us he moved to another part of the state and was living in the basement of a church.

We don't always understand why certain things happen to good people like Earl, but in a book entitled *Why?: Trusting God When You*

Don't Understand by Anne Graham Lotz, she provides some encouraging words:

> *"Trust Him!*
> *Trust Him!*
> *Trust Him when you don't understand!*
> *Trust His Heart!*
> *Trust His Purpose!*
> *Trust Him when your heart is broken!*
> *Trust His goodness!*
> *Trust Him beyond the grave!*
> *Trust Him to know best!*
> *Trust His plan to be bigger than yours!*
> *Trust Him to keep His Word!*
> *Trust Him to be on time!*
> *Trust Him to be enough!*
> *Trust Him to set you free!*
> *Just trust God—and God alone!*
> *When I don't understand why, I trust Him because*
> *. . . God is enough."*[11]

> *"Life's most persistent and urgent question is, 'what*
> *are you doing for others?'" (Martin Luther King Jr.).*

Elvis

Out of the blue, I received an e-mail from a stranger stating his brother-in-law, Fred, from another part of our state, was going to be in a local hospital and requested a visit. He said his brother-in-law had Parkinson's, was mentally challenged, and didn't know anyone in the area. I did not know the person who sent the message or how he knew my name. It was like God sent this person to me for a specific reason.

There were numerous excuses for why I wouldn't visit Fred because, after all, I didn't even know who he was. However, something in my spirit kept telling me I needed to follow up with Fred.

On the first visit, I was a bit nervous and almost decided it was a bad idea to visit a stranger. When I walked into the hospital room and observed Fred, I was moved by compassion. Fred's body was twisted with rheumatoid arthritis, and a heavy black beard covered his face. His look indicated he was just as confused as I was since we had never met.

When I confirmed it was Fred in the hospital bed, I explained I received an e-mail from his brother-in-law and was there to meet him. After a few introductions, Fred asked me a very pointed question, "Does Jesus love me?"

After moving past the shock from Fred's question, I took Fred through the sinner's prayer and told him that God loved him and forgave him of any sins.

On my second visit with Fred, someone mentioned his nickname was Elvis. When I inquired of Fred about this, he confirmed Elvis was his hero. I had a CD of Elvis Presley at home and gave it to Fred at our next visit.

Many visits continued before Fred returned to his home about 120 miles away. When I e-mailed Fred's brother-in-law to ask how he got my name, he did not answer. He only said Fred appreciated everything I did for him. This seemed strange, but maybe it was a request directly from God in Fred's time of need.

"If you let your head get too big, it'll break your neck" (Elvis Presley).

The Marine

A friend, Pete, is a US Marine and served as a sergeant during the Korean Conflict, after which he was awarded two Purple Hearts. Pete is in his eighties, walks with a cane, and enjoys the company of his dog Hammer. I met him one day while he was walking Hammer, and we became good friends. He is a volunteer chaplain at a nursing home.

This US Marine has taken the time to share inspiring stories with me, and he gave his permission to include a few in this book. He worked as an expat for a company in Africa for four years and, as you will read, took on a role he had never done before.

When he first arrived in Africa, he was approached by several church leaders who told him they had been praying for many years for a missionary from the USA. When he told them he was not a missionary but had been sent there by a company as an expat, they were disappointed.

When he walked away from them, he thought about it and said to himself, *If not me, who?* He turned around, and the next words out of his mouth were, "I will." He ministered to that local church for four years while in Africa.

Since he had access to an airplane owned by his company, he and his wife took a short flight to an area not far from his house. During their flight, he noticed a field with numerous old airplanes. He landed his plane and walked around snapping pictures of the old German aircrafts.

The next thing he knew, he felt something piercing his side. It was an African soldier who proceeded to arrest him and his wife. They were told they were on government property and were marched off to an old jail just a block or so from where their plane landed. The soldier locked them in a small jail cell with a stench of urine, making it hard to breathe. Their worst fear was that they would be separated and possibly not see each other again. Pete and his wife were strong believers in prayer, so they passionately asked God for His intervention.

A few days later, early in the morning, a young African man arrived at their jail cell and simply said, "My name is David, and I am here to help you." He was smartly dressed in a blue outfit. He had a ring of keys he used to open the door to the jail. Once they realized they had been freed, Pete and his wife ran from the jail to their airplane and flew home before their exit was discovered.

The US Marine and his wife firmly believed David was an angel on earth sent by God. God continues working in mysterious ways!

Another miracle in this marine's life was when he was in the Korean Conflict. He was a sergeant and led a platoon in battle at Boulder City in North Korea in 1952. One day when the platoon was being fired upon by Korean troops, he saw a large white bird, like an egret, flying overhead with bullets and rockets hitting in the air all around the bird.

The sight of this beautiful bird caused him to stall a few seconds and kept him from being killed. His entire troop of four men proceeded ahead of him over the hill and were all killed. He received two serious wounds, was rescued by the medics, and sent to a hospital in Japan for treatment and time to recover.

He believes, as I do, that the white egret was provided by God to save his life just as He did with Jonah. In Jonah 1:17 (NIV), it reads, "The Lord provided a great fish to swallow Jonah." God definitely had a plan for this marine's life and brought him safely back to the USA.

I also served my country during the Vietnam conflict but didn't make it to Vietnam. God also had a plan for my life.

> "There are heroes among us, not the least of which is the hero in each of us"(Captain Gerald Coffee, US Navy Ret.).

The Fisherman

My wife and I attended a family retreat one summer and this time away allowed for fellowship with friends we knew from our church. We listened to our guest speaker, reflected on God, prayed, read scripture, ate delicious meals, and enjoyed time together.

One morning, our guest speaker's presentation focused on the life of Daniel. Daniel was a man of God who was faithful and worshiped Him regardless of the consequences. When Daniel was cast into the lions' den, the angels held the mouths of the lions closed to keep him from being killed.

After this inspiring lesson, I was talking to one of my friends, who asked if I liked to fish. I said to her fishing was something I used to enjoy doing many years ago. She told me her young grandson would like to fish and wondered if I would take him. He had a fishing rod and the retreat property had a small lake for us to use. I knew the grandson was autistic but agreed to help him fish.

As we approached the lake, I noticed a young man with his fishing rod on the dock. I was not familiar with fishing in a small lake, so I asked the young man what he used for bait. He told me he was using hot dogs because that worked with catfish.

I asked the young man if he would help my friend bait his hook, so he did and threw the line in the water. Just as he handed the fishing pole back to me, a large catfish took the bait and bent the pole in half.

I called for my friend's grandson and handed him the fishing pole with the fish on the other end. He was overwhelmed and started crying, so I took the fishing pole back and gave it to the young man helping us.

When he brought the fish to dry land, he kissed the fish and threw it back into the lake because he seemed to know my young friend was terrified we were going to hurt the fish. Once the fish was safely back in the lake, he was fine.

When the excitement was over, I thanked the young man, and then his mother arrived to check on him. Before we returned to our next session at the retreat, I asked the young man who helped us what his name was, and he told me, "Daniel." As you'll recall, we were studying about Daniel before we decided to go fishing. God had this fishing trip in His control.

Daniel, the young man who was fishing for catfish, was caught caring when he showed compassion and love for the boy who wanted to fish.

> *"People don't care how much you know about them once they realize how much you care about them. Caring is contagious—help spread it around"* *(Harvey Mackay).*

The Janitor

My wife and I usually attend church dinners on Wednesday evenings. Following dinner, classes are available for children and adults.

At one of these dinners, we learned a teacher wanted volunteers to speak with preschool children about being grandparents. My wife and I were asked and agreed to come into the class of about twenty children to speak and answer any questions they might ask.

When we entered the room and were introduced to the class, a young boy said, "I know him," referring to me. I looked at the young man and did not recall knowing who he was. When the teacher asked how he knew me, his answer was, "He is the janitor." When I heard this, I laughed since I had served ten years as a volunteer on Wednesday nights as part of a cleanup committee. This involved moving tables, chairs, taking out trash, sweeping, mopping, etc.

This young boy came to church with his parents for dinner and saw me and others cleaning up each week following the meal. I'm quite sure he had witnessed me with a mop or broom in my hand, cleaning crumbs or a sticky lemonade spill on the tile floor of the eating area.

This was quite a compliment for a volunteer like me to hear this response from a young boy. I felt like I made an impression on him when I responded that I was not a paid janitor but a volunteer helping others. From the mouth of babes comes the truth. I was blessed by this expression and was caught serving others.

"Each day of our lives we make deposits in the memory banks of our children" (Charles R. Swindoll).

Animals on Earth and in Heaven

Two friends, a married couple, went through seminary to become pastors. They received a call from God to create and sell pet sympathy cards. Their full-time pastoral assignments keep them busy, but another passion is caring for abandoned and rescued pets. This couple feels strongly, as I do, that there will be animals in heaven. Animals are like Jesus in their expression of unconditional love. It seems natural to think animals will be in heaven with us, but we know this will be up to God's plans. Revelation 4:11 (NIV) states, "You are worthy, our Lord and God, to receive glory and honor and power, for you created all things, and by your will they were created and have their being." Revelation 5:13 (NIV) states, "Then I heard every creature in heaven and on earth and under the earth and on the sea, and all that is in them, singing: 'To him who sits on the throne and to the Lamb be praise and honor and glory and power, for ever and ever!'" And Jeremiah 32:27 (KJV) tells us, "Behold, I am the Lord, the God of all flesh; is there anything too hard for Me?"

A few years ago, God placed this card project on their hearts, and they worked to create cards with beautiful pictures of animals and a story that went with each animal picture. They produced over twenty different cards, including sympathy, thank you, thinking of you, get well, etc. A portion of proceeds of any sales will be donated to animals and people in need. I knew the couple before they made the decision to attend seminary. Both were working as scientists for a large corporation. They are located a few thousand miles away, but we continue to keep in touch.

The couple kept me in the loop about their project, and I have helped where I can find connections. The cards are displayed in a few places, but sales have been slow. We trust the cards can be available on a website to help with awareness. This is a wonderful project and an opportunity to volunteer. The following is one of their pet sympathy cards:

A compassionate driver saw a cat stranded on the center island of a busy highway. When she got out of her car to help him he was only too glad to jump into her arms. The driver took the cat to our Vet who already had an over abundant supply of cats to adopt. Hearing that this sweet cat was up for adoption, my husband could not resist the temptation to surprise me again. We named him *THOMAS*. He reminded us of Nathanael, a black and white cat we had loved some years before. *THOMAS* is sweet and gets along well with all our cats and dogs. One of his great pleasures is to sit at the window and watch birds use the birdbath. He's happy and playful and truly enjoys life to the fullest. We are so thankful that someone cared enough to get involved and came to his rescue.

www.allcreation.jm@gmail.com

Original Card Design, Photos, Logo and Writings by Jean & Manny Vieira.

A portion of the proceeds from the sale of cards will be donated to aid animals and people in need.

Made in the USA-1

I'm reminded of a black and white, short-haired, tuxedo cat given to me by my daughter. My first name is James, the cat looked like a butler, so it was decided his name would be James Butler or "JB" for short. He was an outdoor cat and a neighbor said he would feed him while we took a vacation. We returned home and could not locate JB. We checked around the neighborhood and ended up at a local pet shelter where we found him in a cage that resembled a jail cell. He saw us and the look on his face was, "what took you so long." He had been rescued.

A few years later, our family moved to another state and my wife brought JB on her flight to meet me. He was in a carryon bag with zippers and he decided to open the zippers with his front paws, escape and make his way to the plane's food galley. A minute or so later, a voice came over the speaker asking who owned a black and white cat now underfoot of a flight attendant. He had been rescued yet again and my wife had to admit ownership. Fellow passengers were still talking about JB when I met my wife at the arrival gate that day.

A short time after we arrived in the new town, JB slipped out the front door during a wind storm. We searched everywhere for over a week, but with no success. My wife and I were attending a business meeting one evening and our daughter was visiting at our home from out of town. She called where we were meeting and said, "Daddy, they found JB!" We went from the meeting and picked up JB. He had that same "what took you so long" look on his face as when he had been found at the pet shelter. He had been rescued again by a young couple who lived about 6 blocks away from our home. They looked at JB's collar which had a tag with our name and phone number from our old location. They called the number, heard the disconnected message and took the time to call telephone information to locate our new phone number. This young couple was caught caring with their special efforts to locate us. We enjoyed our "delinquent" JB for several more years. I think this is how it will be in heaven—seeing our pets again!

Animals show unconditional love, compassion, assist in healing, and, in some cases, provide humor. A funny story is when I met a lady for the first time while trimming bushes in my front yard. We were "caught caring" as we made a concerted effort to find the owner of a lost dog. The car stopped in front of our house, and the lady acted like she might be searching for an address.

The lady told me she lived on the next block and had found a beagle dog wandering around near her house and wanted to know if I was aware of anyone who owned a beagle. Dogs and cats are required to be on a leash, so this dog must have slipped out of a door or an open gate.

Right away, I thought of my next-door neighbor who owned a beagle. The beagle had a reputation of escaping from his yard or house and having to be chased by the owners. The lady and I went next door, rang the doorbell, but no one was at home. As a good neighbor, I confidently told the lady I only knew one neighbor with a beagle and was sure this lost dog must belong to them.

I went with her to her car and helped her lift the beagle. The dog was overweight, but the two of us carried the beagle to the neighbor's house. The homes almost always have block walls around the yards. I suggested we lift the dog and put it over the wall. I went home to get a small step ladder, and we carefully put the dog over the wall. The lady seemed pleased, and I was feeling like a Good Samaritan who deserved a pat on the back. I went back to working in the yard.

It did not occur to me to leave a note on my neighbor's door about finding his beagle. I had almost forgotten the event when my neighbor stopped by for a chat a few weeks later. I began telling him how the lady found the beagle, about knowing it was his dog, dropping it over the wall, and then I saw a strange look on his face. He quickly commented, "So you are the one." I couldn't figure out his reason for looking surprised and saying that.

My response was, "Yes, I was the one. You were not at home, and I forgot to leave a note."

My neighbor began to laugh and told me the rest of the story. When they got home that evening, his daughter went to the back yard to discover not one but two beagle dogs. His daughter ran into the house to tell the parents, and they didn't understand her excitement so went to check it out. After seeing the two beagles, it didn't answer where the other dog came from.

I asked my neighbor what happened next. He said the new beagle did have a collar with the owner's telephone number. The day the dog showed up in the car with the lady, I was so sure it was the neighbor's beagle that I did not think about checking the collar. Our neighbor called the number, notified the family, who soon arrived to pick up the family pet. I would love to know what the two beagles thought about the whole event.

It is important to love your neighbor as yourself but always be careful when rescuing beagles!

> "You think dogs will not be in heaven? I tell you, they will be there long before any of us" (Robert Louis Stevenson).

Heart of My Heart

I have a friend who was diagnosed with serious heart defects, and doctors said his condition was critical. I listened to him describe this negative situation and tried to speak as many words of encouragement as I knew how. He told me his only hope was to receive a transplant.

His age was a factor, and being on a heart-transplant list was going to be difficult. Fortunately, he located a hospital that did not categorize you on your chronological age but used the physical condition of the candidate's body. He qualified and was placed on the list. Many prayers were needed as the wait began.

I sent him a prayer shawl and explained how the group making his shawl prayed while they were knitting or crocheting. As the shawls were completed, they were blessed by one or both of our pastors. He was pleased with the prayer shawl and sent a picture with it wrapped around him, and smiling broadly. This was amusing since he is sometimes a serious person. He informed me he kept it with him all the time, and it was warm, soft, and comforting.

I recall speaking with him early one morning. His words were barely audible, and I realized it was because he was physically weak. His doctor was not optimistic that morning, but God sent him a new heart a few hours later. Surgery went well, and my friend is like a new person. He is totally energized and has new goals and ambitions. God has a plan for his life and is not finished with him!

"Love is a fruit in season at all times, and within reach of every hand" (Mother Teresa).

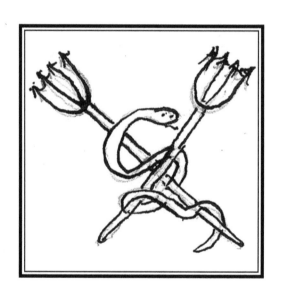

Satan Is Alive and Well!

While living in the Northeast, we were friends with a couple who were fellow church members. The husband was a tennis partner, and we socialized with them regularly. The wife had health issues, and it was not clear exactly what was going on, but we continued to pray. My wife talked to her quite often and tried to encourage her.

One evening, I answered our home phone, and it was the lady calling for my wife. While on the phone, I asked her how she was doing. She excused herself from the phone, and I heard her in the background talking to someone. I thought it was her husband, but as I listened, I heard a strange voice. I never asked her who it was, and she returned to say she was doing fine. I then turned the phone over to my wife.

Several weeks later, my wife picked her up at her house to take her out for dinner. On the way home, the lady began talking in a strange voice and appeared to be carrying on a conversation with herself. My wife, even though she had excellent perceptive skills, was trapped in the driver's seat with this woman talking to someone else. My wife later told me it was as if the woman was carrying on a debate with Satan and wanting answers to questions.

My wife recounted how she prayed, sang spiritual songs, and prayed some more the entire drive while strongly rebuking the evil presence of Satan. In Ephesians 4:26–27 (NIV), Paul instructs us to not be angry "and, do not give the devil a foothold." Upon arrival at the woman's house, she regained her normal behavior, thanked my wife for driving to dinner, and walked away. My wife sat quietly in her car for a few minutes, thanking God for watching over her. In the Bible, we read about Jesus rebuking Satan the time when Satan tempted Him three times.

When my wife told me about this experience, she realized God allowed her to go through this for a reason. It was important for her to be strong in her belief that Satan is alive and well but God is in control.

"Relying on God has to begin all over again every day as if nothing had yet been done" (C. S. Lewis).

Keepers of the Flock and Real Champions

My wife grew up on a large dairy farm, and a friend lived less than a mile away on another farm. For all the decades since, they remain close friends. She's a wonderful Christian woman, a nurse's aide in a care center, and they keep in contact through phone calls and e-mails. She lives near a retirement area and attends a church where some residents go to her church.

When my wife and I got married, we moved to Kentucky, and I was stationed there with the US Army. We became members of a small church in the town and soon got to know our pastor. Our oldest daughter was born two years later, and we requested she be baptized by our pastor. I completed my commitment with the army a few months later, and we moved back to Florida. We corresponded with our pastor for about twenty years but somehow lost his address through either one of our moves or one of his.

We enjoy keeping in touch with former pastors after we've made moves away from the local church and settled in a new city and state. Several of these amazing pastors played vital roles in our spiritual journeys.

One morning a few years ago, my wife received an e-mail from her friend. She recounted to us about inviting a lady to come to her house for dinner, and their conversation after dinner turned to computers and how to work with e-mail. Our friend decided to fire up her computer to give her visitor simple instructions about how the e-mail works. She was showing her visitor the steps to set up an address book for easy e-mail correspondence. She clicked on her address book, and our first names, Don and Velma, popped up on the screen. Her visitor showed a look of surprise and asked our friend to tell her something about these two people. Our friend described who we are, and the visitor could hardly believe what she was saying.

The rest of the story is that her visitor is our former pastor's wife from Kentucky. She and her husband lived in the nearby retirement village. Our friend had worked in a rehab center where our pastor was a patient after having a stroke. Our friend and the pastor's wife attend the same church and had gotten to know each other. Velma's childhood buddy is a person who has consistently put others first and seeks opportunities to help, keeping Christ's commandment to be a *"light to the world."*

Some pastors we keep in touch with have interesting stories:

A. The Bus Driver/Mailman

When my wife and I dated during high school, we did not live in the same neighborhood and consequently attended different high schools. In fact, our schools were rivals in all sports or any type of competition. It just happened that the pastor of Velma's church drove a school bus for extra income. One of his trips each morning was to take a load of kids to my high school. I would write a special love note to my girlfriend, Velma, and give it to the pastor to deliver to Velma. She lived quite a distance out of the city, and his bus route also included her stop. When she was picked up in the afternoon to be taken home, she would answer my note, and I would have a fresh reply the next morning. This went on for about two years before we graduated from high school.

This pastor performed our wedding ceremony. When I completed my military assignment, we returned to be members of the bus driver's church. We continued communicating with the pastor and his wife, and they are in their nineties and are still great role models. The pastor pioneered new churches after his first retirement. When we moved to the southwest, we learned the pastor's brother lived within thirty miles of our house. We got to know the pastor's brother and wife and were blessed to have the pastor and his wife stay with us when they were visiting his brother. As Velma went through cancer treatment, we would regularly receive telephone calls from them to check on Velma's condition.

B. Dapper Dan

A job opportunity necessitated a move to another town. We settled in and found another church where we liked the people, and the pastor was unique. He was not only a great pastor and speaker but excelled in finance. During some weeks, we would arrange to meet for coffee and prayer, and he always had a copy of the new *Wall Street Journal* tucked under his arm. He was well respected for his business acumen and served as a financial consultant for that denomination's headquarters in our state.

This pastor always dressed to the nines. He kept his fashion up to date with his ties, shoes, shirts, coats, etc. His sermons were inspiring and educational. He would use new words in his sermon that had been listed in current issues of the *Reader's Digest*. We attended this church for seven years until we moved a long distance to the Northeast to begin another career.

He was an inspiration to me and a person I considered a role model. We keep in touch with him. We enjoy talking with him on the phone frequently, and he checked on us when Velma was undergoing treatment.

C. The Evangelist

After our big move from the South to the Northeast, we spent over a year visiting numerous churches within an hour's drive before deciding on a church home. We happened to join a local church very close to our home at the same time a new senior pastor was being assigned to that church.

An activity we attended just after joining this church was a Valentine's party. This fun event provided a time to become acquainted with several people. A few weeks later, the new pastor asked us to come in to his office. We discussed some gaps in different age groups in the area of social activities. The pastor asked if we would be willing to put together a committee to brainstorm ideas.

Many members in this church were working full-time and had families at home with full calendars. We learned from experience that if you want something done, ask a busy person, and it will be accomplished. Our goal was to provide good, clean, fun events at the lowest cost possible. Since this group was given the role of filling the gap for fellowship, we took on the name God's Adult Persons (GAP). We had a wonderful committee of creative planners and memorable activities: (a) three separate bus trips to Culinary Institute of America (CIA), most famous in the USA, enjoying dinners in Italian, French, and American restaurants, (b) mystery bus trip to an unknown destination with committee members the only ones with the answer (there were several stops, the destination being a banquet in Portuguese restaurant), and (c) dinner and dancing events with themes for country/Western and 1950s/'60s.

This new pastor was an excellent speaker, and it was evident he gave time and effort in sermon preparation. Those who heard him on Sundays were gifted with a solid nugget of spiritual wisdom to carry home and digest. Almost every week, we would spend time discussing the "nugget" with our daughters while enjoying a meal.

We committed to serving as volunteers in several different roles in that church. When a new, workable idea was presented, the pastor would ask the person with this idea to put together a plan to determine if it could be implemented.

The pastor was out and about visiting in homes of members and prospects. He would usually visit us when he needed us to take on a new role, help with an event, or serve as a committee member. During the almost twenty years as members, my wife and I did agree to be responsible for some challenging assignments.

One evening, he called and asked if he could come by for a visit. He had a request for us to manage a pretty significant event which involved hosting an international clergy person who would be a guest speaker for a couple of weeks. Just prior to him asking us about this new responsibility, he made a statement that we have used as a learning experience for the future. He said, "The Trotters do not know how to say no." We did say yes for him and enjoyed hosting in our home an interesting gentleman from another continent. However, since that evening, we've managed to use no for other volunteer opportunities.

Gretchen Thompson pointed out in her book titled *God Knows Caregiving Can Pull You Apart: 12 Ways to Keep It All Together*, "Often for caregivers, one of the most difficult words to get out is the word 'no.'" One of her colleagues said, "Sometimes you have to choose the smaller negative in order to allow for the larger positive."

In Thompson's book, she says, "of course we can't do everything, and we have to say no."[12] We must be good managers of our time and projects and be realistic about what we can and cannot do.

I have always heard it is better to burn out than to rust out, but I feel it is good to be smart enough as caregivers not to burn out. The pastor was instrumental in introducing us to an organization called the DOC (the Disciplined Order of Christ). The DOC formed in the '40s and had headquarters in Nashville. I was asked to be president of the northeast region, which allowed me to plan and implement ecumenical retreats in our region, covering all the way from Maryland up to Maine.

The pastor who is in his eighties, still uses his excellent teaching skills, and we continue to communicate. These stories are a personal testimony to the fact that God creates *happenings, not coincidences!*

My wife's friend was caught caring when she helped a lady with her e-mails and later discovered the blessings we received because of her actions. Our pastors in their stories were also caught caring for others.

"In helping others, we shall help ourselves, for whatever good we give out completes the circle and comes back to us" (Flora Edwards).

The Brothers

I became a Duet volunteer and have assisted this organization for several years and will provide more details about it later in the book. My assignments are to take homebound individuals to medical appointments. This has been rewarding to me because I can assist individuals who need rides and, at the same time, count my blessings.

One of the first individuals I picked up was a lady who was blind. On our way to a doctor's appointment, she briefly shared her story but quickly changed the subject and talked about what activities she enjoyed and food she liked to eat. As a young high school graduate, she attended training to be a secretary. One day on her way to school, she was the victim of a serious car accident, which resulted in blindness. She gave up her dreams and plans to be a secretary and has been blind and endured multiple operations over the past five decades.

When we arrived at the doctor's office, I took her by the arm and led her to her appointment. She didn't let blindness keep her from enjoying life. I was humbled and thanked God for my many blessings.

A gentleman I'll name Saul was also an assignment from Duet, and I took him to doctor appointments and drove him to church each Sunday. Saul lived with his brother, and they both had Parkinson's disease. His brother owned a car but could not take Saul to all his doctor appointments.

Saul was punctual and was always waiting in front for me when I picked him up for church each Sunday. One Sunday when I arrived, Saul was not waiting. I rang his doorbell, and there was no response. After a few more minutes, I left. However, I made a note to call him after church to see if all was well. I made a call, but there was no answer. I thought about reasons for why he was not home and decided he and his brother might have been called away for a family event or decided to go on vacation.

The next day, I received a call from Duet informing me another Duet volunteer was scheduled to pick up Saul for a doctor's appointment and Saul was not home. I said I would go to Saul's house and do a little checking.

When I arrived at his house, I rang the doorbell several times with no response. I went to the next-door neighbor's house, and she did not know anything about Saul and his brother being away from home.

In Arizona, most homes have a wall around the backyards. I borrowed a ladder from the neighbor and climbed over the wall to be able to look through a glass door or window. I did look in and could see the living room, but there was no sign of Saul or his brother.

With all the action going on at Saul's, another neighbor appeared to inquire about what was happening. I told him the events of the past few days, and he said he had a phone number for Saul's brother's son. To make this story as short as possible, he called the son, who drove from thirty miles away and found Saul and his brother both lying on the floor in different rooms of the house.

Both gentlemen had fallen and could not get to the phone to make a call for help. What would be the odds of both brothers falling and being physically unable to call for help? The brothers had been lying in separate rooms on the floor for five days without food. One brother fell in the bathroom and drank water in the toilet to survive.

We called 911, and both brothers went to the emergency room at a local hospital. When I visited them in ER, all Saul's brother could say to me was, "You saved my life." It wasn't me because God was directing all involved, and teamwork played a big part in the rescue. First, Duet made the call to me, which prompted me to go check on the brothers. Second, neighbors and finally, the brother's son found them disabled in the house. The brother's son told me later he usually makes a phone call to his father every few days to check on him but had been sick with a flu virus and had not had time to check.

All of us that were involved in this rescue were caught caring.

According to Harvey Mackay in his article titled "Things I've Learned in Life" (Arizona Republic, January 11, 2016, Section 10A), "We can't go it alone," and he defines teamwork as "a collection of diverse people who respect each other and are committed to each other's successes."[13] Reprinted with permission from Nationally Syndicated columnist Harvey Mackay, author of the New York Times #1 bestseller "Swim with the Sharks without Being Eaten Alive."

"Be faithful in small things because it is in them that your strength lies"(Mother Teresa).

The Ride

Early one beautiful Saturday morning, my wife and I took off on our motorcycle to participate in a poker run to support a fallen police officer's charity foundation. The young officer's life was snuffed out while coming to the aid of a fellow officer. The annual poker run raises funds to support activities for young people. The riders were all ages, races, and backgrounds.

We quickly headed to our starting location and joined over three hundred other beautiful motorcycles of every make and model with riders dressed in just as many variations of fashion as their bikes. Several three-wheel bikes added to the diversity of the group. Motorcycle riders are known to value opportunities to assist with causes to support veterans and law enforcement. The participants were given instructions about where to position our bikes and made aware of the starting line. Coffee and doughnuts were there for the taking to energize us for the adventure.

When the time came to start, we revved our engine, adjusted our sunglasses and helmets, then took off side by side with another bike. In all the advertisements for the poker run, it was strongly recommended that riders be experienced and competent to always keep control of their bikes. In a situation like this with hundreds of bikes, a lack of good judgment and experience can quickly lead to injuries and even worse. We felt comfortable that all riders were completely capable and had safety as a priority.

At the starting location, the fallen officer's wife, his children, and parents were there to greet us and show appreciation. It was a time to be grateful for life and having the physical ability to be a part of this. For anyone who has never been on a poker run with over three hundred motorcycles, the sensation and excitement is difficult to describe. The loud roar of that many bikes together is almost deafening. Law enforcement escorted us along the highway and stopped traffic at busy intersections to let us pass through, and this added to the feeling of doing something that really counted.

The idea of a poker ride is to go for several miles and have scheduled stops for eating, bathrooms, good conversations, and time to admire one another's bikes. The poker card for each participant is punched when you arrive so you can show your full ticket at the end of the ride as evidence you stopped at each location and completed the entire run.

About halfway through the ride, we pulled away from the mass of bikes to stop at a gas station for fuel. I did not want to get away from the city and run out of gas in a remote location. We drove away from the service station, and I ramped up my speed to about fifty-five miles an hour to reconnect with the large group of bikes. We had only gone a short distance when I glanced to the right and noticed something moving in an open field. I thought it might be a coyote and did not think too much more about it until I felt something slam into my right foot. I was able to release the throttle to slow down the bike and looked down to see that my brake pedal was bent so badly that it would not work. I managed to pull the bike to the median on our left and used the front brakes to completely stop. I held the bike up with my left leg but could not put pressure on my right foot.

It all happened so fast, and I looked to make sure my wife was okay and we were far enough off the busy highway. It took a minute to collect my thoughts, but as I looked down, I saw a beautiful large dog weighing perhaps sixty pounds. It was the same object I had seen in my peripheral vision racing in the vacant desert. The combination of the dog's speed and the bike's fifty-five miles an hour caused quite a thud. Unfortunately, the dog was killed on impact. It looked very healthy, did not have identification, and must have been lost from its owner and frightened by the tremendous roar coming from the bikes.

We could not stay where we were and did not want to leave our bike on the side of the highway. I was in a lot of pain but managed to use my left foot to keep the bike upright. We were familiar with the area, so we calculated a shortcut to ride home as quick as possible. I used my front brakes, and we took our time going on side streets to reach our house. We looked at the injury to my foot and went to the emergency room near our house. My right foot had a clean break, and the doctor prescribed a boot for six weeks, and it healed.

Looking back at this ride, I have thought how fortunate we were to end up with only a broken bone. We were riding in the far-left lane of a four-lane busy highway. This was how we could immediately pull into the median and avoid being hit by traffic behind us. Another factor was if the beautiful dog were even a second faster, it would have resulted in me hitting the dog with my front tire and perhaps losing control, being thrown off the bike, and possibly both me and my wife being seriously injured or killed. I thank God for protecting us during this ride.

We never know from day to day what will happen, but know that God watches our starts and stops. We were glad we had an opportunity to participate in this ride to show our respect for our dedicated law enforcement officers.

"God not only orders our steps; He orders our stops"
(George Muller).

Sweet Strawberry Ice Cream

A good friend and his wife attended my same Sunday school class. One Sunday, he shared a story I will not forget. He told the events about a friend whose family owned a bakery. He and his friend visited the bakery, then the ice-cream section inside the bakery. Both boys were ten years old and quietly picked up quart-sized containers of strawberry ice cream. To avoid being discovered by his friend's grandfather, they proceeded down a flight of stairs to the basement and into a walk-in freezer to eat the ice cream. They were very still and did not talk while enjoying sweet strawberry ice cream until all the lights in the freezer went off, and they heard the loud click sound of the freezer door being locked.

In total darkness, they stumbled around in the freezer until they reached the door and discovered the handle did not turn from the inside to open the freezer. It was panic time as they realized they were trapped and could not call for help. This happened late on a Friday, and unless someone came in the next few hours, they would be there until Monday. Both boys attempted various ways to free themselves from this prison, but nothing worked. They paced around the freezer to keep warm and then discovered a few paper bags. They wrapped the bags around their arms and legs.

While shivering in the cold, they also found a container on a shelf with something that felt warm. They later learned his friend's grandfather had put some warm gravy in the freezer for future use. Both boys took turns passing the bowl of gravy back and forth to keep warm. They prayed together and asked God to forgive them for stealing the strawberry ice cream as they fell asleep holding on to each other.

An hour or more in the freezer the boys suddenly awoke, startled by the sound of the freezer door opening, only to discover Mr. Miller, the father of his friend, who came to rescue them. His friend's family missed him when it came time to sit down for dinner. His father decided to return to the bakery to search for him since he remembered a glance of them there earlier in the day. My good friend at the age of eighty said his guardian angel must have been watching over him and his friend. He promised not to ever steal, and he doesn't want to eat any more strawberry ice cream.

A few folks in our Sunday school class got their heads together and decided it would be nice to share this story on a wider scale. A friend volunteered to interview the gentleman and wrote his comments in a narrative format. We made several inquiries with Christian magazines and got a response from the magazine *Angels on Earth*. The story was published with the title "The Ice Cream Thieves" in the magazine (May–June 2010, pp. 18—22).[14]

> *"There is nothing on this earth more to be prized than true friendship" (Thomas Aquinas).*

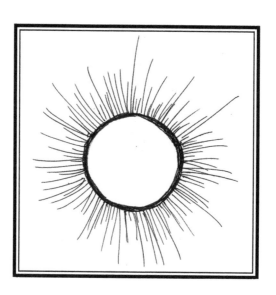

Everything Is All Right

While visiting an elderly gentleman at a rehab center, he told me he did not want to have to die to get to heaven. This seemed rather strange to me since he is retired clergy. His exact words were, "I don't want to go through what Jesus went through to get to heaven." Of course, I missed the real point of what he was attempting to tell me. My quick response to him was that Jesus died for our sins, and we do not have to die a painful death like Jesus to reach heaven. Can you picture a layperson trying to tell a retired pastor the plan of salvation? That was laughable.

When I returned home to share what our elderly friend's fear was, I realized just what I had missed when he was sharing with me. I knew he loved life, and despite being an "elderly" person and having serious health issues, he simply did not want to die. In Psalm 89:48 (NIV), it says, "What man can live and not see death, or save himself from the power of the grave? Selah."

When Jesus died, he was buried and three days later, arose from the grave so that we have a risen Savior. Just as Jesus died for our sins, if we believe in Him, we will die and be with Him in heaven. This elderly gentleman who told me he didn't want to die like Jesus to get to heaven is ninety-seven years old and wants to continue living his life until he sees Jesus in heaven. It's a well-known fact that Christian believers die once (physically) and live twice (once on earth and once again in heaven with our Lord).

> *"Do not let your hearts be troubled. Trust in God, trust also in me. In my Father's house are many rooms; if it were not so, I would have told you. I am going there to prepare a place for you. And if I go and prepare a place for you, I will come back and take you to be with me that you also may be where I am" (John 14:1–3, NIV).*

However, God warns us to not go down the wrong path as an unbeliever.

"But the cowardly, the unbelieving, the vile, the murderers, the sexually immoral, those who practice magic arts, the idolaters and all liars—their place will be in the fiery lake of burning sulfur. This is the second death" (Revelation 21:8, NIV).

Our family is blessed with relatives who have deep, personal relationships with God. My wife's large family meets each year in Tennessee for a family reunion. I am reminded of my wife's grandpa who lived to be ninety-nine years old. His family had been busy making plans to host a large family gathering to celebrate his one-hundredth birthday. They were disappointed when he died seven weeks prior to the big day.

I became acquainted with grandpa shortly after my wife and I were married. He was a dairy farmer in Tennessee all his life and knew the importance of hard work but enjoyed every day. He was likeable, with a smile always on his face and a twinkle in his eye. He had a special way of capturing and holding your attention to the point that you wanted to be with him. We had great fun when we would visit while I was in the military. His farm was only about four hours away from where we lived, and we would visit as often as possible. His wife had passed away early the year we were married, so I never had the opportunity to meet her. They had ten children, seven of which were daughters, so one was always available to cook for him. When it was time to eat, he would say something like, "Don, the girls have the food on the table, let's eat!"

During one of our visits, he told my wife and me he was dating three ladies and needed my wife's opinion about who he should marry. A little background is needed here to let you know my wife was special to him since she was born on his birthday. He was an eligible bachelor who wore overalls and red suspenders. To top it off, at the age of eighty, he drove a new car so he could be in style to date three ladies.

My wife agreed to meet his lady friends, and he arranged for each of them to come to his house on separate occasions so they could be checked out. They did not have a clue and would have been horrified if they had known they were going through an interview. After the introductions and quizzing sessions, my wife told him her favorite. He looked at her with a slight grin and a twinkle in his eye and said, "She is also my favorite." Soon after, he proposed to the "selected one" and they were later married.

Prior to marriage, he wanted to travel to visit his son and family and asked if I would drive him in my car. I could take vacation time from my military job and said yes. My car was an English Ford Anglia with only forty-six horsepower under the hood and would go top speed of sixty miles an hour. We spent the night with him, got up at 4:30 a.m., had a small breakfast, and were ready to go. When we looked outside, it was raining cats and dogs, but we managed to get into the small car with all our luggage. I turned on the engine and started the windshield wipers. It was just a few seconds later when the windshield wiper on the driver's side flew off. He looked at me with that twinkle and a smile and said, "Don, what do we do now?" We made it to a service station down the road and bought new windshield wipers.

Grandpa was a teetotaler who never had a drink and was proud to share that with anyone who would listen. As he reached about ninety-five, he had a difficult time with sleep issues. He went to his doctor, who advised him his circulation in his legs would improve and he could sleep better if he would have a glass of red wine before he went to bed at night. He reluctantly agreed and began to drink a little glass each night before bedtime. A few months went by, and the glass of wine was tasting good. When I saw him the next time, I asked him over dinner how much wine he could have before bed, and he responded with a smile and a twinkle in his eye, "The doctor told me that I should have one glass before bed each night, but he didn't tell me to limit the size of the glass."

Her grandpa was a good Christian man who loved God and blessed other people with his fairness, honesty, showing others he cared. Just seven weeks before he turned one hundred, he closed the smiling, twinkling eyes for the last time, and we all knew that everything was all right.

In James W. Moore's book titled *You Can Get Bitter or Better*, someone asked him, "What is heaven like?" His response was, "All we need to know is God is there!" His book referenced a story by John Baillie. "John told of an old country doctor who made his rounds in a horse drawn carriage accompanied by his dog. One day, the doctor went to visit one of his patients who was critically ill. 'How am I, doctor?' the man asked. The doctor replied, 'It doesn't look good.' Both men were quiet for a while. Then the man said, 'what's it like to die, doctor?' As the old doctor sat there trying to think of some words of comfort to offer, he heard his dog coming up the stairs. Because the door was shut, the dog began to whimper and scratch at the door." The doctor said to the man, "You hear that? That's my dog. He's never been in this house before. He doesn't know what's on this side of the door, but he knows his master is in here, and so he knows everything is all right. Now, 'the doctor went on.' 'Death is like that. We've never been there, and we don't know what's on the other side, but we know our Master is there. And because of that, we know everything is all right.'"[15]

> *"The moment we take our last breath on earth, we take our first in Heaven"* (Billy Graham).

The Blessings of Music

In the book *Why Good Things Happen to Good People* by Stephen Post and Jill Neimark, it states, "According to Eric Roter, an emergency room physician and master cellist, not only is singing creative, but it's a very physical process, and when you're making music, your body responds as if you were giving it a physical work-out." Stephen Post and Jill Neimark write in their book, "Singing can also be therapeutic according to a long-term study co-sponsored by George Washington University and the National Endowment for the Arts. Begun in 2001, the project follows participants in community arts programs who are ages sixty-five to one hundred, like the Senior Singles Chorale. Compared to a control group of the same age, 'the singers feel physically healthier, visit the doctor less often, have fewer falls, and are more involved socially, less depressed, and in better spirits.'"[16]

I played the clarinet in my high school band and have not continued to participate in any band since. Velma enjoys being active in vocal music and recalls her family always had a strong interest in music. Her mom was an exceptional pianist who never had a formal music lesson. Her dad sang in male quartets as a bass, and her siblings sang vocal parts to form a double quartet. In early years, she sang with children's choirs. In high school, it was acapella and regular choirs, constantly busy performing concerts. As an adult, she joined ladies' groups, church choirs, ensembles, etc.

A few years ago, she and about twenty-five others helped in forming a community choir which blossomed into over one-hundred members. After each concert, the choir director invites attendees who enjoy vocal music to consider checking out the choir. The choir has been invited to sing for local sports events and traveled and performed around the United States in Hawaii, New York's Carnegie Hall, Lincoln Center, and a Disney location. They've traveled outside the continental USA to places in Europe. The ages of choir members span from the twenties to nineties. This large group recognizes the importance of caring for one another. When Velma was plodding through all her treatments, she was blessed with many from the choir who showed their love, prayers, and support.

The medical reports for Velma have been good since completing treatments, and she attends weekly choir rehearsals with performances sprinkled in. The choir members do not hesitate to share their joys and concerns with one another, and we consider them part of our family.

In this large group, there are the challenges of illness, loss of family members, divorce, separation, personal disappointments, and requisite need for a healing touch through hope and love. The song "Why We Sing" by Greg Gilpin has provided encouragement and sense of belonging for choir members, and most concerts include it as a finale. According to Greg Gilpin, singing is "a sound of hope, a sound of peace, a sound that celebrates and speaks what we believe, a sound of love, a sound so strong." This song says, in Greg Gilpin's beautiful choice of words, that music can be like excellent medicine for our souls. The verses and refrain are as follows:

"Why We Sing (Words and Music by Greg Gilpin)"

"A sound of hope, a sound of peace, a sound that celebrates and speaks what we believe. A sound of love, a sound so strong. It's amazing what is given when we share a song. This is why we sing, why we lift our voice, why we stand as one in harmony. This is why we sing, why we lift our voice. Take my hand and sing with me. Soothe a soul, mend a heart, bring together lives that have been torn apart. Share the joy, find a friend. It's a never-ending gift that circles back again. This is why we sing, why we lift our voice, why we stand as one in harmony. This is why we sing, why we lift our voice. Take my hand and sing with me. Music builds a bridge; it can tear down a wall. Music is a language that can speak to one and all! This is why we sing, why we lift our voice, why we stand as one in harmony. This is why we sing, why we lift our voice, why we sing, why we lift our voice. Take my hand and sing with me. Take

my hand and sing with me. This is why we sing! This is why we sing! We sing! We sing!"[17]

> *"There is nothing in the world so much like prayer*
> *as music is" (William Shakespeare).*

Coincidences?

I met a gentleman while attending college who was born the same day as me. Other coincidences piled up from that point since he worked for the same company, and we both had been granted a leave of absence to complete our education. The little bit of difference was he had worked at the corporate headquarters, and I was employed at a satellite location. Another point to ponder: he was also an only child like me.

Before we met on the college campus, we didn't know anything about each other. Another divergent was his birthplace was West Virginia, and mine was Tennessee, but on the same day. He happened to be interested in science as a subject, and I liked anything to do with math. Being from company headquarters, he knew quite a few of the same people I knew, but we had never crossed paths until we met in a college class.

It only took a short time for us to become friends, and we shared time together in the campus library studying together. Our plans for the future were quite similar: to complete our respective degrees and return to the company after graduation. These plans were not to be fulfilled because we both decided to keep going with education, complete our master's degree, and neither of us returned to the company we had worked for. He veered in his course work toward secondary education, and I decided on higher education to enable me to teach at the college level.

After graduation, we kept in contact for many years even though we moved out of state and I started another corporate job. Our two families were young, and we called each other every year on our mutual birthdays. He was a big country music fan, and one year, he mailed a record by Jerry Lee Lewis titled "Thirty-Nine and Holding," which I still have.

My friend was always joking, and I thought he would have been a famous comedian or movie actor. You never needed to be concerned about what to talk about when you were in his company. I remember an incident when both families had been out for a social event. We were all riding in his van, and he stopped at a local store to buy cold drinks for all of us. He just happened to overhear a conversation about someone who had been killed nearby in a small plane crash. From listening, he learned enough about the person in a short amount of time that he felt like he knew him personally. When he returned with the cold drinks, he shared what he had heard.

We drove away from the convenience store and traveled to a section in the road that had been blocked by local law enforcement. He asked an officer what was going on and was informed the area was closed because of an airplane accident. Being quick to recall information he learned in the little store, he spoke to the officer as if he knew the victim, "Too bad about Lou." His wife was surprised, but she knew he was using his sense of humor to make all of us laugh.

The same day, we decided to go to another town for a picnic. He was driving an orange VW van, and I was driving a green sedan. When our families got in their separate vehicles, we somehow went in opposite directions. I thought I was following his orange VW van but later learned when I tried to pass the vehicle that it was not my friend and his family. I turned around, went back to the point where we started, and a few minutes later, he pulled up in his orange VW van. He realized he had been headed in the wrong direction and decided to return to our original starting point. We both greeted one another like nothing had happened and proceeded on our family adventure. It was just a small bump in the road for our daylong family adventure. Who would have thought that there would have been two orange VW vans traveling so close together?

For years after being several states away, we were in close touch. We had numerous family near where he lived and made a visit with him and his family while on our vacation. He informed me on our visit that the doctors scheduled back surgery, and he would be checking in the hospital the next day. We wished him well and continued our trip to see family in another town. The next day, we learned he had a massive heart attack and died. He obviously had heart issues that had not been diagnosed, and I was sad to know he passed at a young age.

To continue with the coincidences in our two lives, it was necessary for me to have bypass heart surgery just a few years after my friend passed away, and I am diligent in my annual cardiac checkups. It is clear that my friend was a part of my life for a reason, and I will be forever grateful we crossed paths. He made me a better person, and his education gave him an opportunity to teach special-needs students. A sermon I heard many years ago was titled "There Are No Coincidences, Just God Instances."

> *"Learn to get in touch with the silence within yourself, and know that everything in life has purpose. There are no mistakes, no coincidences, all events are blessings given to us to learn from."* *(Elizabeth Kubler-Ross).*

Friends Are a Gift from God

In Mark 12:30 (NIV), Jesus gave a clear description of the greatest commandment. He said, "Love the Lord your God with all your heart and with all your soul and with all your mind and with all your strength." He went on to further say, "The second is this: love your neighbor as yourself, and there is no commandment greater than these." I am sure that God knew if we loved our neighbor as ourselves, friendships could blossom and grow.

The story of David and Jonathan (Saul's son) was a perfect example of true friendship. In 1 Samuel 18:12 (NIV), it says, "Saul was afraid of David because the Lord was with David but had left Saul." King Saul was jealous of David and plotted to kill him. Because of Jonathan's friendship and love for David, "Jonathan said to David, whatever you want me to do, I'll do for you" (1 Samuel 20:4, NIV). "The two of them made a covenant before the Lord. Then Jonathan went home, but David remained at Horesh" (1 Samuel 23:18, NIV).

The true friendship was extended after Jonathan was killed in battle, and David became King of Israel. He told Mephibosheth (Jonathan's crippled son from an early age), "Don't be afraid . . . for I will surely show you kindness for the sake of your father Jonathan. I will restore to you all the land that belonged to your grandfather Saul, and you will always eat at my table" (2 Samuel 9:7, NIV).

My wife is always repeating the statement, "In order to have friends, you need to be a friend." It is apparent that both David and Jonathan were a friend to each other and had to work at it to remain friends. This is especially true since Jonathan was the son of Saul who desperately wanted to kill David.

In John 15:15 (NIV), Jesus calls those who believe in Him friends: "I no longer call you servants, because a servant does not know his master's business. Instead, I have called you friends, for everything that I learned from my Father I have made known to you." And in John 15:13 (NIV), Jesus's friendship was so strong that He was willing to die for our sins: "Greater love has no one than this, that He lay down His life for His friends."

We have been blessed with many friends over the years, but I give credit to my wife for keeping in touch with friends through various modes of communication (e.g., special cards, telephone calls, and e-mail). There's no possible way to mention friends and relatives from all places we've lived, but I do want to mention a few.

A dear friend was a senior partner in the same law firm where my wife was employed as a legal assistant. He was well established in his practice and highly respected with clients and colleagues. If a client was not in a financial position to pay the chargeable fee for professional services, he would willingly reduce the charge. The law firm was successful, and each employee worked long hours to make it grow. The partner's wife and daughters became friends of our family, and this relationship has remained firm throughout the years.

The additional reward we received was the expanded view of a friend who was concerned about our other family members. He graciously counselled with our family to ensure all necessary legal documents were up to date. Their children were similar in age to our daughters, and we shared trips to Disney World, simple picnics, and family travels. He always encouraged me on my journey to pursue and attain my college degree.

After a few years of classes and finally completing my goal, I was employed with a university. This allowed me a couple of months of time for other interests. He knew I wanted to keep active and offered me a part-time consulting position with his family's real estate business. The summer months of employment benefitted us financially and gave me an opportunity to become knowledgeable about sales and real estate.

Another close friend is Dorothy (Dot) La Motta, who is mentioned in the acknowledgment section of this book. Dot was instrumental in proofreading my book. My wife met Dot at work, and Dot helped guide her through the maze of unwritten corporate norms, rules, and regulations. The large corporation was dramatically different from her years of being employed in private law firms and even civil service employment. She carpooled to work with Dot, and they became good friends while sharing their lives on the road to corporate bliss.

A few months after meeting Dot, she invited us to visit them and have dinner together. That was quite an experience since we were greeted at the door by two very intimidating Great Danes. We saw their heads at the window and could not believe they were only pups. This visit was an opportunity to meet Dot's husband, Lou, a very outgoing, gentle Italian man. He was a person who didn't seem to ever meet a stranger. We went on to experience the most delicious Italian meal we have ever had in our lives. We thought the first course was the entrée but found out it was only the beginning of one appetizer, and more followed. We knew then we were converts to good Italian food, and it has remained that way. Dot was an expert in cooking and enjoyed entertaining in her beautiful home. Dot and Lou also bred and exhibited Great Danes at professional dog shows along the East coast. They both held officer positions in their dog club and bred several beautiful champions over the years.

Dot and Lou, in addition to full-time careers, both became emergency medical technicians (EMTs) on their local rescue squad after moving to a new town. They took turns with other volunteers to be on call in life-and-death situations. They were professionally trained, state certified, and loved giving back to their community and to others who needed help. Years later, we heard stories of various rescue missions that sometimes happened in the middle of the night. They were confidential and never revealed names or addresses—just sharing situations.

While discussing experiences, Dot and Lou shared how intense the EMT training was and how excited they were to pass the state exam the first time. But during their months of medical study, they both discovered just how serious this volunteer job was when they were faced with certain situations. One night in her frustration, Dot wrote a poem about how they felt during their months of training. I'm sure anyone who serves on a rescue squad will relate to some of the medical terms; others could just enjoy the poem and its bit of humor. The captain of the rescue squad had this poem engraved in calligraphy on a wooden plaque, and it still hangs in the community room of their rescue squad.

"On the Road . . . to EMT
Dot La Motta (1979)"

I moved to a town, no friends did I know,
I wanted some action, so where should I go?
The Rescue Squad lured me, a hero I'd be
Those flashing red lights and that sirens for me!
My work never brought me in not a dollar
The only thing padded was the cervical collar
I just took a course called 'EMT 1'
No time left for movies, no time left for fun
My nose in a book, my glands all a'sweat
When I pass this course, an emblem I'll get
I struggled with traction, I learned CPR
And now extrication from a smashed up car
It's a whole new world of strange words and phrases,
This week is a test, never make all these pages!
Contusions, abrasions, avulsions galore
What else will they teach me, there's room for no more
My mind is a jungle of medical facts
Must I flex that neck, or splint that back?
I sometimes think of the things that were funny
Like our intimate moments with Annie the dummy
Oh, when will the end come, when will it be
Am I a flunked out Joe or an EMT?
When we're on a call, we do our darnest
to preserve the life that's placed upon us
The grateful family with their heartfelt pain,
gives a humble 'thank you' nere to see us again
So with all that I learned and all that I do,
I did meet new friends like I wanted to
But the best friend of all is not to be seen
He alone helped me reach my dream
I can only offer a humble nod,
And say from my heart, "THANK YOU GOD."

Dot has amazing efficiency in marketing and writing. She's not a professional editor but was willing to share her skills of proofing and suggestions. She resides in North Carolina, but if we could talk her into it, we would love to have her nearby to continue adventures and be a part of our care ministry team.

Knowing her, she would probably write a poem about our wonderful volunteers and the lives they touch every day. So here's to a friendship that has lasted more than thirty-five years.

As they say, some friendships are for a short time, others for a season, and others a lifetime. Looks like we're in for the long haul.

Dot gave me permission to share the following personal story she wrote:

"The Teacher behind Bars: A Healing Journey
by Dorothy La Motta

I was a different kind of teacher on a journey that would lead me behind bars. I had no degree, no classroom, no principal to report to, no grading papers and no assigned working hours. What I did have was a passion for learning, teaching and encouraging people. My journey started one day when my mentor at Bible study invited me to go into a local prison and teach a lesson from our prison ministry booklet. Though a little apprehensive, my desire and curiosity conquered my fear as I agreed to take on my first challenging assignment.

Entering the prison was both nerve wracking and exciting, but also reassuring having my mentor with me. We walked past the massive brick walls topped with menacing barbed wires three feet high and cameras everywhere following us like the paparazzi. A towering lookout station with an armed deputy peered down on us. We waved a weak hello. In the dingy front entrance, we surrendered our driver's license and car keys and took a stroll through the electronic body scanner. While we were waiting, the check-in deputy was on his computer, checking us for any outstanding warrants, tickets, or other offenses. Moments later, we were escorted down a maze of hallways devoid of any color, pictures, or paintings. Each massive steel door we went through slammed behind us, locking us in with the prisoners. Only the deputy had the security electronic device that controlled the doors and elevators.

The prisoners, knowing we were coming, gathered together willingly in a large room. We were welcomed with big smiles and friendly greetings. Nearby, a deputy was stationed watching all of us with the eyes of an eagle and a gun within inches of his trigger finger. As I gazed at the twenty-five inmates, most were young with unsightly hairdo's, others shamefully too old to be there, some toothless and either emaciated or extremely obese. Some looked hardened by their years of physical or mental abuse, repeated incarcerations and addictions. Yet in their desperation for momentary escape from their cells, they were happy to see us. To them, we were a breath of fresh air, always bringing in a big smile, good news and hope to their sad lives, broken hearts and regrets. Teaching prisoners was challenging enough, but during our God moments, they educated me on the horrors of street life. Drugs, alcohol and prostitution got them lured into a world of sinful pervasiveness as they spiraled downward listening to wrong voices. Soon they made immoral and illegal decisions that hurtled their destiny to incarceration. The more I heard, the more I knew I was meant to be a teacher behind bars and help to brighten their imprisoned lives with hope for their future. We laughed, we cried, we sang, and we prayed together. Happily, I saw many inmates come to a close relationship with the Lord.

The biggest challenge of my life occurred six years later. One of the police officers on the men's prison ministry asked me if I would consider mentoring a twenty-two-year-old unwed lady who killed her infant boy. He said she was under psychiatric care and had already served part of her sentence. She was now in a halfway house and in need of a spiritual mentor. I learned that she threw the baby down on a cement patio and then tossed him in a pool to ensure his demise. My initial response was one of reluctance and a bit of judgmental attitude mixed in. With a knot in my stomach, I accepted the challenge. The big day came when I had to meet her. As I waited in a glass-enclosed private room of the psychiatric unit, I envisioned a hardened, tattooed toughie sauntering through the door smoking a cigarette with a cocky attitude. Instead, a very attractive, nicely dressed blond with flowing long hair entered the room. She had a friendly smile, a soft feminine voice, and a graceful walk. As she was still under psychiatric evaluation, I sat close to the wall with the panic button within reach. Better to be safe than sorry echoed through my mind. I was told not to mention her crime or ask questions about it as it could spark some hysteria, anger or other emotions. We exchanged a few pleasantries, and our first meeting went well.

Soon, I was getting more comfortable stepping outside my comfort zone mentoring a convicted felon. Slowly, my judgmental attitude began to change as my heart started to soften. As I was teaching her, God was teaching me to be more compassionate, more loving and understanding. She will live with her experience forever, but it wasn't my job to judge her. My assignment was to help her overcome her grief and bring her hope and encouragement while strengthening her faith in God.

Weeks later, she began to confide in me on her own about her wrong friends and how she fell prey to witchcraft rituals and mind-altering practices. As I listened to her heartbreaking story, I had to fight back my tears. Her downward fall led her through years of unimaginable grief, family pain, incarceration, intense psychiatric care, repentance and finally believing in God. Soon our relationship grew each week in trust and confidentiality.

Months later, I began receiving letters and poems from her expressing her gratitude and appreciation for my weekly visits. God put her in my life to melt my judgmental attitude and love a person for who she was inside, not for what she did. While she grew in faith, I grew in wisdom. While she faced a brighter tomorrow, I faced another life-enhancing challenge. We parted company after two years with hugs, tears, and a final prayer. She was later released on probation, but not without knowing the promises of God to strengthen her walk into a new, exciting future.

What did I learn from this challenge? I learned to be more compassionate when I couldn't understand the why behind the crime. I learned that I could face an unusual challenge surprisingly well when I allowed God to journey with me and do His will in my life. And lastly, I learned that bad things happen to good people, but during it all, God teaches us a lesson that brings us closer to him.

So, I encourage you to step outside your comfort zone with your skills, knowledge, or passion. Be an inspiration to someone out there waiting to hear your extraordinary experiences, stories, and testimonies, which could propel others to try their own life-enhancing challenges.

Then you can mark your own mental report card Assignment Completed—A+."

In Matthew 25:35-36 (NIV), Jesus said,

"For I was hungry and you gave me something to eat,
I was thirsty and you gave me something to drink,
I was a stranger and you invited me in,
I needed clothes and you clothed me,
I was sick and you looked after me,
I was in prison and you came to visit me."

Another friend was raised in a small town in South Carolina. He and his family moved near us in another state, and we got acquainted. There were three daughters with similar age to our daughters. We had common interests, and it was a joy to be around his family. He was in the construction business and took time to help others like me learn these skills. We both had enduro motorcycles and spent time as families going on dirt-bike riding adventures. There are many stories that could be told about hours out in the Florida hot sun riding our dirt bikes until exhaustion won, our endurance was depleted, and too many layers of dirt made us end our day with laughter and fun memories. I still have a motorcycle and enjoy riding. My friend is a marine and proudly served his country and continues to live the marine motto, *"Semper Fi" (Always Faithful)*. You might recall in the beginning of the book, I mentioned a marine who had the nickname "Do What?" This is the same man.

My marine friend and I became like brothers. Proverbs 18:24 (NIV) says, "A man of many companions may come to ruin, but there is a friend who sticks closer than a brother." A sad time for all of us was when his youngest daughter was diagnosed with a life-threatening disease. She was married and had to endure operations over a period of several years. She was in a hospital in Virginia shortly before she passed, and her parents had come there to be with her. Knowing she had limited time on this earth, she asked her dad what heaven would be like. He told her he was not real sure, but if she went there before he did, she should go to the first shade tree she came to and sit down and wait for him to meet her there. I'm quite sure she remembered what he said and is waiting under that tree for her dad.

When I began my first college teaching job, we moved again to another town. Being new and not knowing very many people, a great couple in our church "adopted" our whole family right away, and we became friends. We had fun times together with a large group of people about our same age going on picnics, meeting at restaurants and church events. The gentleman taught adult Sunday school classes, and he reflected on God's love in his life. He had a passion for sharing his research and knowledge about the book of Revelation. A few years before he passed away, he completed a book with his thoughts about Revelation.

Moving on to another state provided new adventures and possible opportunities to make new friends. A wonderful couple we met were former military and experienced numerous moves around the country during an exciting career. We were fortunate to get to know them, and our friendship grew over the years. We had much in common, they were eager to seek new, unchartered adventures and were always willing to drop what they were doing to see new places in Arizona. The wife, Sharon, is an artist and is the person I mentioned earlier as the designer for the book cover and sketches in the book.

Two other friends were instrumental in keeping us from getting homesick. Our two daughters were married, had their own children, and were living in other states when we made our long-distance move to Arizona. Without any family members in the immediate area, these friends saw we needed to join up with their large family for Christmas in the Southwest. We've experienced local and international travels together to some beautiful places.

A sweet lady from Texas showed a warm and friendly welcome to us when we visited a church in Arizona. This warm Southern hospitality helped us emotionally and spiritually to return and be a part of this congregation. Our friendship continues with times together in fellowship and food (she loves to cook so occasionally shares extra meals with us). Another example that friends are a gift from God!

An unexpected joy I received was an e-mail from a childhood and early-adulthood friend in Florida. We kept in touch after marriage and even through years in the army. The years passed with Christmas cards until about sixteen years ago, when communication stopped. His wife found an old e-mail address for us and sent a cryptic note asking if we would answer. We talked on the phone and are now making plans to get together as soon as it can be arranged. Our day-to-day activities become so time-consuming and could be better spent cultivating stronger relationships and new blessings.

The list of good and faithful friends is long and could go on and on. Moving around several times from state to state, it has been a highlight for us to keep great friends. According to Mother Teresa, "The true way and the sure way to friendship is through humility, being open to each other, accepting each other just as we are, knowing each other."

We were all caught caring by simply being a friend and keeping in touch with one another over the years.

Being a part of care ministry provides opportunities to reach out with care and concern to someone who may have had friends in the past but desperately needs a friend today.

> *"I would rather walk with a friend in the dark, than alone in the light" (Helen Keller).*

Love

When we think of love, we usually think of our immediate family, which would include our spouse, parents, siblings, children, grandchildren, and so on. A former pastor told his son when he was heading off to college to remember *who* he was. This impressed me since I knew he was asking his son to always know he was loved as he embarked out of the nest and into a world of challenges and temptations. It reminded me of a bird being pushed out of the nest and the bird's mother whispering, "Remember lessons taught and be safe on your own." We are blessed with two wonderful daughters and sons-in-law, who have given us five grandsons. My wife and I have had similar experiences as the pastor did with his son. Both daughters went out of state for education, and we recall asking them to remember who they were.

The pastor's comment to his son also took me back to when I was going off to join the US Army just after completing high school. My mom told my dad I would never live at home again, and her young son was gone forever. I thought it a little strange at the time and told Mom not to worry since I knew I would certainly return home after my enlistment and live in the family home. What did I know? I got married after one year in the military and never returned home again. Her concern for me let me know that I would be missed and that I was loved by my parents.

In 1 Corinthians 13:3 (NIV), Paul talks about the importance of love. "If I give all I possess to the poor and surrender my body to the flames, but have not love, I gain nothing." 1 Corinthians 13:4–7 (NIV) also states, "Love is patient, love is kind. It does not envy, it does not boast, it is not proud. It is not rude, it is not self-seeking, it is not easily angered, it keeps no record of wrongs. Love does not delight in evil but rejoices with the truth. It always protects, always trusts, always hopes, always perseveres." And 1 Corinthians 13:13 (NIV) reads, "And now these three remain: faith, hope and love. But the greatest of these is love."

As we continue to think of love, the greatest unconditional love can be seen when God gave His only Son to die for our sins. John 3:16 (NIV) says, "For God so loved the world that He gave His one and only Son, that whoever believes in Him shall not perish but have eternal life."

An article by Randy Kilgore titled "You Missed the Chance" was published in October 27, 2016. In this article, there are two believers in Christ who are discussing a controversial issue, and their opinions are different. When the discussion is over, the older person appears disinterested and states, "I don't know what it is you want." The younger man replied, "You missed the chance to love me" and went on, "In all the time you've known me, what has seemed to matter most to you is pointing out what you think is wrong about me. What do I want? I want to see Jesus—in you and through you."[18] We pray others will see Jesus in our lives not for our glory but for His glory!

I can think of similar examples to Randy Kilgore's story when certain individuals have not shown they "like" me. I take time to ponder these cases and may be guilty of rationalizing (e.g., Do I look like someone this person doesn't care for? Did I do something unkind to this person, etc.)? I know I've been guilty of not always expressing compassion or love to everyone, and reasons may be the same in reverse. Randy points out the need for acceptance and prayer for others. If we fail to love others or have them love us, just as the young man said to his older Christian friend, "You missed the chance to love me."

"Love is when the other person's happiness is more important than your own" (H. Jackson Brown Jr.).

My Cup Runneth Over

A career move to the Northeast opened new opportunities for me to volunteer in our community, including church and my work. With a background in college teaching, I was asked to be on an advisory committee for a local nontraditional college. It was a win-win for both of us since it allowed me to stay focused on higher education, and I added value to their institution. The relationship with the college continued for a period of twelve years.

My involvement with the nontraditional college opened another exciting adventure. The college nominated me to be an advisor for the American Council on Education (ACE) in Washington, DC. Three years later, I was appointed as a commissioner for ACE. This nomination was a first from the industry work area since the others were in academics from various universities.

The evolution continued as the appointment to ACE then led me to be able to work as a volunteer with one other commissioner, a professor from the University of Wisconsin. It was a great experience to be on his team and offer high-potential leadership programs to outstanding professor candidates at land-grant Universities throughout the United States.

Without a doubt, blessings and good fortune flowed my way, enabling me to give my time to help others. The important benefit of these opportunities was that I received more than I ever gave. I learned in giving your time to help others (regardless of how small) doors can open to greater adventures in the future. Proverbs 11:25 (KJV) says, "The liberal soul shall be made fat: and he that watereth shall be watered also himself."

In an article entitled "Make Service an Integral Part of Your Life" in *Don't Sweat the Small Stuff and It's All Small Stuff*, author Richard Carlson states, "When you give, you also receive. In fact, what you receive is directly proportional to what you give."[19] Also, in another article from the same book titled "Do Something Nice for Someone Else—and Don't Tell Anyone About It," he suggests, "One should give for the sake of giving, not to receive something in return."[20]

It seems volunteering is receiving more press time in society and the community today. In an article in the *Arizona Republic* dated July 15, 2014, titled "Volunteering: A Noble Way to Receive a Varsity Letter," students can be awarded a varsity letter for volunteerism. This Big Volunteer on Campus (BVOC) was created by the Gilbert Education Foundation for volunteerism at Campo Verde and Highland High Schools in Arizona and expanded into all the district's schools.[21]

For an individual to volunteer a service, it requires internal motivation. The person needs an underlying motivational factor (e.g., family interest, desire to give back, or maybe simply a good heart). The reward is doing a good job helping someone because you desire to be a good Samaritan.

The motivation to volunteer is quite different from being paid to do a service and knowing there will be a check forthcoming for your efforts. This book's purpose is not to discredit or diminish a person who works full-time to receive a salary but to consider benefits involved from using volunteers who are passionate about what they do.

Brad Formsma, in his book titled *I Like Giving*, tells us, "Doing something generous without anyone telling you to is so exhilarating it becomes addictive. You'll want to do it again. And Again."[22]

It is my opinion that the ideal situation would be an individual volunteering to serve others while working full-time for a salary. The best volunteers are people who take the time from busy schedules to assist others. This, of course, includes both retired and employed people. Volunteerism is applicable to many organizations (e.g., churches, Boy and Girl Scouts, nonprofit organizations, or just your neighbor who may need some help).

"A life not lived for others is not a life" (Mother Teresa).

Challenges

On a visit with my parents in Florida, I went out in the early morning for a jog. Upon returning home, I realized my left arm was throbbing with pain. I didn't give it too much thought since the weather outside had already reached ninety degrees and probably close to 90 percent humidity. My daughter was also traveling with me and visiting my parents. She was a pharmaceutical representative for a major company and expressed concern when she heard me mention my arm had been throbbing. She knew my primary care physician and quickly looked up the office number and called to arrange an appointment for me.

The doctor's appointment was scheduled for just a few days after returning home. My primary doctor referred me to a cardiologist after looking at changes on an EKG. The usual procedures included a stress test and later a heart catheterization. Results from the cardiologist were surprising to me; his recommendation was heart bypass surgery. I thought this might be erroneous since I was in good physical condition. He challenged me to go for a second opinion, so I consulted with two more cardiologists and received the same diagnosis.

The surgery was scheduled, and we had a nice visit with friends the night before. They shared an excellent book, *Bypassing Bypass: The New Technique of Chelation Therapy* (a non-surgical treatment for improving circulation and slowing the aging process) by Elmer Cranton, MD. This was not great timing, but they had very good intentions.

I learned a valuable lesson from this life-changing surgery. Being a physically able adult, I still had to ask for help. My family and friends came to my rescue and reinforced the idea that it is easier to give than receive. I did accept help and received a blessing of care and concern from others. This experience also gave me better insight in situations for others who need help.

There is an interesting article in the February 2014 issue of *Psychology Today*. The article "Intimacy, A Path Toward Spirituality 5 Reasons Why Receiving is Harder than Giving" by John Amodeo who cites, "Receiving is often more difficult than giving." He goes on to say it is because "we fear intimacy (disallow ourselves from receiving a gift and/or a compliment). We have to let go of control (when we give we are in control). The fear of receiving because there may be strings attached. The belief that it is selfish to receive. Finally, wondering what they want from me."[23]

In another part of Brad Formsma's book *I Like Giving*, he mentions, "Receiving can be harder than giving, because receiving reminds me that I need other people. If you are going to become a good giver, it will serve you well to become a good receiver too."[24]

On a beautiful, cool Sunday afternoon, my wife and I dressed up to attend a hosted dinner to celebrate volunteers. We parked our car in the resort's garage and started the incline up two levels of steps to the restaurant level. As we walked, I observed my wife walking much slower than usual. I asked what was wrong, and she said she was having difficulty breathing. Knowing our location, we thought about a hospital just a few miles away. We got back in the car and headed for that hospital's ER. All the training we attended for CPR always recommended calling an ambulance. In this situation, we knew an emergency vehicle would be at least five minutes away, so God sent along some of His angels to guide us where we needed to go.

Upon our arrival at the hospital, we found the ER empty, and my wife was taken care of right away. She was given oxygen for the breathing and inserted a PIC line for medication since she has small veins. We were there for the rest of the day, and the doctors discovered a mass behind her breathing area. The small hospital was not equipped to handle her situation, so they made inquiries at other local hospitals. She was transferred by ambulance to a larger hospital, and another angel guided us to the right place for treatment.

The hospitalization for my wife turned out to be two weeks with only one of those days outside the intensive care unit. There were almost daily procedures and tests conducted to determine her medical treatment options. The specialists diagnosed it as non-Hodgkin's lymphoma. The doctors kept my wife in a semiconscious state until her breathing was back to normal. The day she was fully awake, she heard this beautiful prayer on a broadcast system:

"Open our ears to the needs of others, Lord.
Let today be our chance to really hear what is being
said by those around us.
Grant us patience, openness and compassion so we
will be eager
To understand others' needs. Perhaps they just need
to be heard.
Maybe they will need comfort, or they might need to
know Your goodness.
After listening, may we speak words that are of
You and intended for that particular person.
Never let our own objectives override the conversa-
tion You intend.
We ask this humbly. Amen. (Author unknown)"

The diagnosis for my wife would begin a new life journey we had never traveled before, and it seemed like an eighteen-wheeler truck had run over us.

The doctors said in cases of non-Hodgkin's lymphoma, the oncologists might recommend chemotherapy be administered first and then possible radiation. My wife's situation was different, and she urgently needed to reduce the size of the mass with radiation. The CT scan after several radiation treatments in the hospital showed they were working, and she was given a discharge to go home.

The doctors scheduled outpatient treatments once a week to complete the prescribed fifteen radiation treatments. The radiologist was very thoughtful and kept us informed about her progress. Her next CT showed the mass much smaller, and she was then ready for the oncologist.

The oncologist explained the chemotherapy and wanted her to begin treatments. We were aware of side effects from chemo and talked about the possibility of a cure being worse than the disease. We both have a strong faith in God and know He is in control. The oncologist reviewed her tests up through radiation and recommended a new drug that was in the trial stage be added to the chemo cocktail. We agreed to the trial drug since it showed potential. We were given a list of side effects, and neuropathy was near the top of this list.

She was handling the chemo treatments well until she finished the fifth one. Neuropathy in hands and feet had progressed, and the oncologist decided to make a change in her cocktail. The oncologist prescribed medication for the neuropathy and began researching the next steps for her chemo treatments.

God continued to watch over us, and we received help and prayers from church friends and members of care ministry and many good wishes from faraway friends and former pastors. We can't say enough about the importance of friends when experiencing an illness or loss.

When her blood levels were good, chemo began again, and she completed the prescribed seven treatments. A PET scan followed and then another meeting with the oncologist. He gave us the good news: she was clear of cancer and in remission. She met with the radiologist, and he confirmed the news. We were thanking God for guidance and grace in answering our prayers. We firmly believe and say to all who will listen, God is still in the miracle-working business. Doctors and modern medicine are a part of this miracle.

Prior to receiving feedback on the PET scan, I had spoken to a good friend and asked him to pray for good results. After we met with the doctor to discuss the PET scan, I called my friend to thank him for his prayers. When I called, he told me he had been taking a nap shortly before I called. He had experienced a dream where he was in a group of people singing "Blessed Assurance" by Fanny Crosby. He said he dreamed his voice was louder than the other singers', and instead of singing the usual words "perfect submission, all is at rest," he was loudly singing "perfect remission, all is at rest." When I spoke with him on the phone and said she was in remission, he said he already knew it and proceeded to give me more details about his dream. I firmly believe this was confirmation of how God works through the prayers of His people.

She continues to take medication and has physical therapy for neuropathy. The non-Hodgkin's lymphoma for her seemed to be a fast cancer, so PET scans are done every three months during the first year to determine if there is any reoccurrence. She has had good results, and we praise God!

A few months before my wife's diagnosis, we received a phone call from our pastor asking if we could attend a training class about starting a cancer support group. Both pastors had been invited, but their schedules were too busy for them to attend. This was a two-day pilot training class, and it was excellent. We returned home and began thinking about who would be a good fit as a support group coordinator.

The pilot class we attended was just three months before my wife's diagnosis. I'm not one to think God puts roadblocks in your path but do believe God has a plan for each of us. We now feel God wants us to be the instruments to begin a cancer care group in our church. Several months after my wife's report of being in remission, we were invited to attend a refresher training course from the same organization. When we returned home from the second training, we trained eight people in our church to be cancer care ministers, and they are now functioning on our care ministry team at church. More will be said about this ministry later in the book.

"Hold everything in your hands lightly, otherwise it hurts when God pries your fingers open" (Corrie ten Boom).

As we journey into the next chapter, the focus is on change, leadership, teamwork, and encouragement (CLTE). These key components are necessary in helping you move forward with a project, initiative, or running a committee such as a care ministry team. Moving forward will provide you with some tools and suggestions necessary in the design and implementation of a care ministry team.

CHAPTER 3

Moving Forward: Change, Leadership, Teamwork, and Encouragement (CLTE)

"The righteous keep moving forward and those with clean hands become stronger and stronger" (Job 17:9, NLT).

In addition to having a caring heart and attitude when helping others, it is necessary to be aware of and include change, leadership, teamwork, and encouragement in your mix. All four of these are essential when designing and managing a care ministry team.

Change

According to Ken Blanchard and Phil Hodges in their book titled *The Servant Leader: Transforming Your Heart, Head, Hands & Habits*, "Change is a given. It will happen. Your organization will adapt or die."[25]

In a book by John P. Kotter (Harvard Business School) titled *Leading Change*, he points out in order to make change happen, you need to "build a coalition that can make change happen. This requires finding the right people, creating trust and developing a common goal," that can be shared by the team.[26]

James W. Moore, in his book *You Can Get Bitter or Better!*, writes about a lady who just lost her husband. "I don't know how I'm going to make it without him," she said. "But I know one thing: I have a choice to make! I can get bitter or I can get better. And I have come to the church because I want to get better!"[27]

Dr. Robert Schuller was a pastor and author. He wrote *Don't Throw Away Tomorrow* and emphasized the phases we go through in life as beginning to end, and the end is a new beginning. In new beginnings, there's toddlers and on through teenagers, young adults, middle age, senior citizens, and even death. Schuller assures us even death is a new beginning in eternity: "If you maintain a positive attitude toward every ending experience, you can turn every ending into a beautiful beginning."[28]

Since change happens regardless of the situation, we should put a positive spin on change and become a change agent. According to Dennis Stevenson, a corporate consultant, as stated in his blog dated April 15, 2008, he explains how it feels to be a change agent:

- "Lives in the future, not the present.
- Is fueled by passion, and inspires passion in others.
- Has a strong ability to self-motivate.
- Must understand people."[29]

Tommy Spaulding states in his book *The Heart Led Leader*, "Whatever your job, title, or role, a passionate belief in what you do is often the difference between success and failure."[30] As situations arise, it is necessary to be willing to step out of the box and be willing to make a change in a new direction.

James W. Moore also wrote in *You Can Get Bitter or Better!*: "Bend a little, and then bounce back! Don't get bitter – get better!"[31]

If you think about the functions involved in committees, the members need to be innovative and reach beyond past traditions to attempt new ideas. We know ideas that worked in the past may not be appropriate and guaranteed to work in the future. By changing one step or procedure, it may make a project easier and will save time. In other instances, the window of opportunity may pass you by, but something entirely different may require new skills. A change agent must always be flexible, embrace change, and make it happen. The Human Synergistics International has given their permission to recommend the following assessments that can help with development and training in this area:

"ACUMEN® Leadership WorkStyles™ (LWS)
http://humansynergistics.com/products-services/
LeadershipDevelopment/LeadershipWorkStyles

AMA DISC Survey™ http://humansynergistics.com/
products-services/IndividualDevelopment/AMADISC,

Perceptive Communications®
http://humansynergistics.com/products-services/
IndividualDevelopment/perceptive-communications.

Leadership

A multitude of styles of leadership exist that may be applied in a situation. Warren Bennis and Burt Nanus point out the difference between management and leadership in *Leaders: the Strategies for Taking Charge*: The problem with many organizations, and especially the ones that are failing, is that they tend to be overmanaged and under led. Bennis and Nanus tell us the definition of management and leadership: "To manage means to bring about, to accomplish, to have charge of or responsibility for, to conduct. Leading is influencing, guiding in direction, course action, opinion. The distinction is crucial. Managers are people who do things right and leaders are people who do the right thing."[32]

David B. Yoffie and Michael A. Cusumano in their book titled *Strategy Rules*, sees Bill Gates, Andy Grove and Steve Jobs as "masters of strategy and surprisingly effective organization leaders." The two write, "Based on our long study of Gates, Grove and Jobs, we have deep respect and admiration for all three leaders, but we do not see them through rose-tinted glasses." "Nonetheless, we believe Gates, Grove, and Jobs were three of the most successful CEOs and strategists in the high-tech world, and perhaps of all time. They set long and short-term goals for their companies, positioned their organizations for success, led teams that executed with ruthless efficiency, and dominated the competition for an extended period of time. While their successes (and failures) are in the past, the lessons they offer are timeless."[33]

John Kotter gives us more direction about leadership in *Leading Change*, stating it is important that a leader "walk the talk, or lead by example." Dr. Kotter tells us, "Often the most powerful way to communicate a new direction is through behavior."[34]

It is important to note that a leader does not have to be skilled in all the details of a project. A good leader knows how to work with people to get a job done.

On the other hand, a leader should not micromanage or attempt to oversee all details. When there are talented people on a team with specific responsibilities, it is necessary to allow them the freedom to perform the job without constant interference from the leader. Leaders can be more effective when encouraging ownership by members to accomplish the job instead of trying to do everything themselves.

According to John C. Maxwell, *Encouragement Changes Everything: Blessed and Be Blessed,* "Leaders can win the confidence, trust, and friendship of the people they lead by taking the spotlight off of themselves and putting it on others."[35]

One of my favorite quotes is from Tommy Spaulding's book *The Heart Led Leader*. He states, "Leading from the heart means leading with love. In this context, love is simply an unselfish and genuine concern for the good of others."[36] He continues, "What business schools and traditionalists have often dismissed as 'soft' skills or people skills are, in fact, often the most important skills a leader can possess. And they are skills all of us can develop and use, regardless of our background, personality or position."[37]

All these principles in leadership apply not only to business but to areas of church committees such as care ministry. Those with the right skills and knowledge should be recognized and promoted into leadership positions.

In one of my jobs, I had the opportunity to work with midlevel high-potential managers. The company identified these high-potential managers in the business unit, and their names were placed on a "promotable list." Once declared high potential, each person was scheduled to attend an assessment center. They were evaluated and given feedback on strengths and weaknesses based upon certain business acumens. The assessment center used a variety of tools and methods to determine strengths and weaknesses, and it all worked on a pass/fail basis. After participants received the feedback, the results were given to the high-potential manager's boss. In the recommendations, it indicated whether the participant passed or failed by listing his/her strengths and weaknesses. After the boss reviewed feedback, the boss could decide if the high-potential manager should remain on the promotable list. Because there was always the risk of being taken off the promotable list, high-potential managers would come up with many excuses why they could not attend the assessment center.

Since the old assessment process did not always work as it should, the managers saw a change was necessary. High-potential managers were invited to attend a diagnostic center in place of the old assessment center to be aware of strengths and developmental areas instead of weaknesses. The exercises were like the old center, but feedback was given only to the participant, and they were encouraged to share with their boss (not a requirement). The diagnostic center didn't function with the pass/fail feature but provided training recommendations in developmental areas while still on the promotable list. As the diagnostic session closed, the high-potential managers were provided feedback, and a career path was developed with the center's specialists. The career path did not have to be shared with the boss, but many high potential managers still on the promotable list were excited about sharing with their boss when they returned.

I believe leadership is the development of people on your team. You should be willing to take members with current strengths and developmental areas and attempt to improve skills through training and job rotational experiences. With a well-planned career path, improvement, and ability can be measured. As steps are accomplished, the career plan should be routinely updated.

A leader must have good interpersonal skills and be a person who motivates and energizes others. This can be demonstrated by becoming a mentor and trainer. A good leader should have the ability to adapt personality and behavior to a variety of people and situations.

A leader should be a team player and be able to make work enjoyable for others. When meeting up with people, a hello in the morning and offering a word of encouragement will mean a lot. A leader should be respectful and encourage input from the team. Human Synergistics International has given their permission to recommend the following assessments that can help with development and training in this area: Coach—Co-Achieving (Copyright ©2016 by Human Synergistics, Inc. Used by permission). http://human-synergistics.com/products-services/ManagementDevelopment/coach---co-achieving

Teamwork

A few of my favorite quotes about teamwork include the following: "Alone we can do so little, together we can do so much" (Hellen Keller, 1880–1968), "Individual commitment to a group effort—that is what makes a team work, a company work, a society work, a civilization work" (Vince Lombardi, 1913–1970), and "If everyone is thinking alike, then somebody isn't thinking" (General George S. Patton Jr., 1885-1945).

In Ecclesiastes 4:9–12 (NIV), King Solomon wrote, "Two are better than one, because they have a good return for their work: If one falls down, his friend can help him up, but pity the man who falls and has no one to help him up! Also, if two lie down together, they will keep warm. But how can one keep warm alone? Though one may be overpowered, two can defend themselves. A cord of three strands is not quickly broken."

Teamwork involves a group effort to be more effective than just an individual. A team consists of members who possess different skills and experiences who can contribute to quicker decisions with better solutions. The process can be "brainstorming" sessions where team members express their thoughts and ideas spontaneously and are displayed either on a white board or paper. After careful consideration of pros and cons of each, a leader and the team progress to elimination of ideas that are either not doable or unfeasible. They then focus on those remaining to thrust a project forward. An important key is to ensure members communicate with each other and share ideas and progress.

Harvey Mackay, in an article titled "Things I've Learned in Life," states, "We can't go it alone. Teamwork is a collection of diverse people who respect each other and are committed to each other's successes. The beautiful part of teamwork is that it offers us the opportunity to use our own special talents and abilities."[38] Reprinted with permission from Nationally Syndicated columnist Harvey Mackay, author of the New York Times #1 bestseller "Swim with the Sharks without Being Eaten Alive."

It is sometimes necessary to provide team learning. Peter M. Senge, Art Kleiner, Charlotte Roberts, Richard B. Ross, and Bryan J. Smith cover this subject in *The Fifth Discipline Fieldbook: Strategies and Tools for Building a Learning Organization*, "Team learning is transforming conversational and collective thinking skills, so that groups of people can reliably develop intelligence and ability greater than the sum of individual member's talents."[39]

John Maxwell wrote *Encouragement Changes Everything: Bless and Be Blessed* and states, "To improve your team, lift up your teammates. Team members always love and admire a player who is able to help them go to another level, someone who enlarges them and empowers them to be successful."[40]

Every team will experience team members who are reluctant to speak up or share their thoughts and members who willingly express themselves. A good leader knows how to engage all the members so they will contribute. There are tools, exercises, and games available to assist in helping a team be more effective in group discussions and making decisions.

According to Tommy Spaulding in his book titled *The Heart Led Leader*, "Everyone's contribution is critical. And the sense of accountability and trust demonstrated by the team's leader builds the foundation and shows the way."[41]

In his book *Forming, Storming, Norming, Performing*, Donald B. Egolf, tells us, "Tuckman, B. (1965), Developmental Sequence in Small groups, Psychological Bulletin 63, 384–399, saw four stages of group development: forming, storming, norming, performing."[42]

> *"In Stage 1, Forming, group members are concerned with orientation matters. Members try to find the boundaries of the group by testing. What are the behavioral limits? In addition, members think about leadership and followership and who will fill these roles. In general, the climate is affable and the group is in equilibrium."*

> *"In Stage 2, Storming, interpersonal conflict emerges. Group members may be upset with the mere fact that they are tied to a group. They may dislike the people who emerge as leaders or they may feel the approach to the task is all wrong. The interpersonal conflict does affect task accomplishment for if two members dislike each other, they will tend to criticize each other's ideas as well."*

> *"In Tuckman's Stage 3, Norming, ingroup feeling and cohesiveness develop, new group roles and rules evolve and are adopted, and group members are more open in their expressions of opinion. The group begins to operate as a group."*

> *"Finally, in Tuckman's Stage 4, Performing, the group's interpersonal conflicts are resolved. This allows the group to focus its energy on the task and its completion. Equilibrium is achieved."*

Teamwork can become a part of our daily lives regardless if it is a care ministry team or a project team at work. Every person has his/her skills, talents, and experiences and the final product can be better if everyone contributes to the solution.

Human Synergistics International has given their permission to recommend the following assessments that can help with development and training in this area: Team Building Situations and Simulations.

(http://humansynergistics.com/products-services/
TeamBuildingSimulations/SurvivalSeries),
(http://humansynergistics.com/products-services/
TeamDevelopment/GroupStylesInventory)

Encouragement

According to a quote by John C. Maxwell, "If you are a leader, you should never forget that everyone needs encouragement. And everyone who receives it—young or old, successful or less-than-successful, unknown or famous—is changed by it."

Joel Osteen states in his book titled *Every Day a Friday—How to Be Happier Seven Days a Week*, "Everyone wants to be appreciated. We love to be valued, to feel encouraged." He referred to Mark Twain, who said, "I can live for a whole year off of one good compliment." Joel continued, "Get in the habit of building up those around you. When you sow those seeds, God will make sure you go higher, too."[43]

In Acts 4:36 (NIV), it reads, "Joseph, a Levite from Cyprus, whom the apostles called Barnabas (which means Son of Encouragement), sold a field he owned and brought the money and put it at the apostles' feet." It's my thought that we should all try to be a Barnabas and be an encourager for others.

A quote from Celeste Holm goes, "We live by encouragement and die without it—slowly, sadly and angrily."

In 1 Thessalonians 5:11 (NIV), it states, "Therefore encourage one another and build each other up, just as in fact you are doing." Everyone needs to be encouraged from time to time regardless of how strong and courageous they are. In 1 Thessalonians 5:14 (NIV), Paul says, "And we urge you, brothers, warn those who are idle, encourage the timid, help the weak, and be patient with everyone."

In Hebrews 3:13 (NIV), it says, "But encourage one another daily, as long as it is called today, so that none of you may be hardened by sin's deceitfulness."

In the book *Encouragement Changes Everything: Bless and Be Blessed,* John Maxwell states, "To encourage people is to help them gain courage they might not otherwise possess – courage to face the day, to do what's right, to take risks to make a difference. The heart of encouragement is to communicate a person's value."[44]

Tommy Spaulding, in his book *The Heart Led Leader,* states, "Heart-led leaders realize that encouraging others is a game-changing opportunity, both for the leader and for the person who is encouraged to do something great."[45]

A close friend has been an encourager for me over the years. He lives his life as a Christian model for me to follow, and he walks the talk. He told me one day he committed to reading the Bible all the way through seven times a year, and at the time, he had a full-time job. He emphasized a need to include Bible reading even if we have busy schedules.

When he mentioned his commitment to his reading the Bible, I had not read the Bible cover to cover. It was my feeling I knew the Bible because of being a part of a church my entire life. I made a commitment to read the Bible all the way through in one year. And now, after eight years, I read the Bible twice in one year. Because my friend encouraged me to do this, I am more knowledgeable about the Bible and it has changed my life!

Everyone needs to be encouraged regardless of their expertise and role in life. The care ministry team is made up of people with a passion for what they do, but also regularly need encouragement from the pastors, chair people, and other coordinators and members of the church. The *CLTE* steps listed above can be applied to major projects, including the church, business organizations, and committees such as care ministry.

In our next chapter, "A Model for Serving Others," you will go on a deeper journey where a place of service becomes a place of joy. As more doors open and opportunities become available, you will find your place of comfort where your discernment, faith, and talents blossom and where you become a valuable volunteer.

This care ministry model was developed and implemented several years ago, on a small scale, and has expanded to twenty ministries where people are caught caring.

CHAPTER 4

A Model for Serving Others

Change – Leadership – Teamwork – Encouragement

*"Each one should use whatever gift he has received
to serve others, faithfully administering God's grace
in its various forms" (1 Peter 4:10, NIV).*

After receiving the call from the pastor to chair a care ministry team, my head was filled with questions, and I felt like Moses at the burning bush, wondering when Aaron was going to show up (Exodus 4:10-16). I considered my skill set and knew I didn't have experience in care ministry. I remembered God wants us to love Him with all our heart and our neighbor as ourselves. I also knew God would provide strength to honor this request. My answer turned out to be yes.

It was time to plan and strategize about a starting point. After more time spent in prayer and counsel with the pastor, my wife and I met with two of our good friends who were longtime Stephen Ministers. Both had wonderful backgrounds in care ministry and were helpful as my wife and I developed and implemented the care ministry team model. The model is based on a simple premise—riding a bike. Once you've ridden a bike, you never forget.

Handling change means stepping out of the box and being open to new ideas. In Acts 9, we read about Saul of Tarsus being changed on the road to Damascus. Saul, the persecutor of early Christians, became Paul the evangelist.

As we worked further with our Stephen Minister friends, the model became a bicycle wheel with many spokes. The center of the model and the pedals represent the chair of a committee or team. The chair is the main point of contact and works hard, pushing forward and empowering coordinators in their individual ministry. Each spoke represents a ministry with a coordinator, who may have twenty or more volunteers assisting in that ministry.

The chair can also be one of the coordinators for a ministry. In addition to chairing our care ministry team, my wife and I are coordinators for several of the ongoing ministries.

Prior to the completion of our design, a good friend of mine at church passed away, and it became necessary to move forward with care ministry, ready or not. My friend was in his forties and experienced a massive heart attack while sleeping. Since he was a single man, his mom and dad asked if there was help available to go through household items and help them make decisions.

We continued assisting for a couple of months until his home was empty and it could be put on the market. My friend's parents purchased an automated external defibrillator (AED) for the church in memory of their son. This purchase spurred on a part of the design for our team.

It's always a surprise what can be accomplished even if you are not quite ready when God is working by your side. We now felt like we could take new steps for a final design. Rev. Dr. Mike Kerr-Osman, Senior Pastor, Dove of the Desert United Methodist Church, has given permission to include the model and process (development and implementation) of the Care Ministry Team in this book. Here's how it worked:

1. A mission statement for our team:
    "The Care Ministry Team promotes wholeness in mind, body and spirit. The service of love is directed to all in need." In identifying who we are, the members of the team have a strong love for God and passion for their areas of support. They find new and innovative ways to provide excellent care and compassion to the congregation and seek opportunities to reach out beyond the walls of our church and to our community.

2. Puzzle pieces of ministries:
   New and old ministries were put together under the umbrella of the team, and coordinators were assigned to each ministry. As in most churches, there are ministries functioning on their own and not reporting to a committee or council. With a coordinator appointed, each ministry became a spoke in the wheel of the team.

3. If a need arises for a new ministry:
   A new ministry requires extra effort and will need to be developed and implemented. Our team is an ongoing and developing process. It is important to start small based on the current needs of the church or organization and expand a step at a time. The AED is just an example of creating a new ministry. The spokes we have on our wheel are the following:

   a. Emergency medical (CPR/AED). As mentioned, the AED was a donation from my friend's parents. We have established a schedule for CPR/AED training every two years for our team, all ushers, and any other interested people in the church. We post names and date of training in a booklet that is kept above the AED. There are three services each Sunday, so names and pictures are listed by service time. If an emergency arises, it is easy to locate those individuals who have received the proper training.

   b. Blood pressure screenings. It was established to have a registered nurse available on one Sunday of each month to screen blood pressure. This person is in a designated room after each of the services. People are encouraged to have regular blood pressure checks (which are confidential) and be aware of any issues.

   c. Community blood drives. The team has sponsored blood drives on our campus for church members and those in the community.

d. Immunization clinics. The team has sponsored immunization clinics for our congregation and those in the community.

e. Health awareness information. The team has resource people available for the following areas: diabetes and Alzheimer's support. The resource people are trained in their area and provide research and information as needed.

f. Prayer line/prayer partners. The team and the congregation volunteer to be a part of prayer partners to be available for prayer. Members and friends leave prayer requests on a telephone line 24/7. The prayer partners listen and pray for each request.

g. Congregational cards. The coordinator sends a get-well, sympathy, or thinking-of-you card when prayer requests are left on the prayer line or concerns are shared from the pastors or office. This ministry was started very early at the inception of the church.

h. Care/prayer notes. The coordinator orders and maintains an inventory of care/prayer notes. The notes are displayed in church's narthex for all ages. The care notes include information on a variety of subjects (e.g., family pet, cancer support, aging, grief, health care, notes for teens, hospice care, etc.). The pamphlets are available free of charge. This is a confidential way to provide beneficial information to people in need.

i. Prayer shawl ministry. The prayer shawls are handmade by members and friends of the church. They meet as a group every other week. As a shawl is created, the individual maker prays for the individual who will receive it. They ask the Lord to give blessings, courage, strength, wisdom, healing, and joy. As they are completed, a pastor blesses each shawl. The shawl wraps the individual in warmth, knowledge, and hope for God to be near and hold them in His loving arms. The scripture used is: "Therefore I tell you, whatever you ask for in prayer, believe that you have received it, and it will be yours" (Mark 11:24, NIV). The shawls are given to individuals who are experiencing life changing events.

The group makes afghans each year for confirmation students and blankets for newly baptized infants or children. The ministry has brought comfort and care to members and friends, reaching beyond the walls of our church to the community. Nursing homes or care facilities, along with multiple other organizations, have also received some of the over one thousand prayer shawls made and given away.

j. Funeral reception. The coordinator has a team of volunteers who provide refreshments or meals following memorial services. Each event is managed as specified by the family. Volunteer ushers are also provided for the service.

k. Hospital and home visitation (pastors and care ministry). The team has a coordinator for management of hospital and visits to the homebound. The pastors are first to make a visit to someone in a hospital, and it is followed up with visits from someone on the team. Volunteers are also responsible for delivering flowers several times a year to the homebound when flowers are donated for a holiday or special event.

l. Homebound communion. The coordinator has a communion kit (grape juice and wafers) and elements are blessed by the senior pastor each first Sunday of the month. The coordinator schedules appointments with homebound individuals to provide communion at least once a month. If a pastor or other persons learn of anyone requesting communion, the coordinator is notified. A report of visits is provided to the chair of the team.

m. Casserole brigade. The casserole brigade provides a meal or meals when there is illness, tragedy, or death in a family. There may be a need for meals when out-of-town relatives or friends arrive to support a family who has experienced a loss. Compassion with a purpose of preparing and serving food is the mission of this group. Volunteers in this ministry are all ages, from teens to elderly. Meals for families can consist of favorite recipes prepared from scratch or already-prepared food purchased from a takeout restaurant or grocery. The coordinator gathers information to determine when and where meals can be delivered to the family's home, a care center, or to a family friend who will manage delivery. When a need arises, the process is accomplished through the coordinator reaching out to volunteers through phone calls, texts, and e-mails.

n. Baby brigade. The baby brigade serves families with new babies. Many years ago, the casserole brigade handled this responsibility. It became apparent as new babies were born that a special ministry was needed for younger families. The process for helping these families is similar to the casserole brigade, and the two ministries can overlap and help each other when more support is needed.

o. Pet care ministry. The primary mission is helping no-kill animal shelters in the nearby area. In just a short few years, over 2,500 food items and supplies and $5,000 in cash were donated to these rescue organizations.

This ministry provides activities for the church and community to enhance pet owners' relationships with their pets. A "blessing of the pets" service is held each year and has included demonstrations by our local police organization's K-9 division. At the blessing service, a pastor or assigned individual blesses each pet and a certificate is given along with a treat. A "remembering our beloved pets" is scheduled every other year for those who have lost a pet. If a pet passes away, there is a volunteer who sends a pet sympathy card and a pamphlet with encouraging content. A six-week dog obedience training class was held for church and the community.

p. Grief support group. The coordinator schedules meetings twice a month with discussion time or a social event. If a member or friend experiences a loss, a series of four booklets printed through Stephen Ministries and titled *Journeying through Grief* are mailed over a period of eleven months after the loss.

q. Job support. The coordinator assists the person with known individuals in the congregation who may be willing to provide contacts in the industry where they are seeking employment. If a resume is out of date or needs development, the coordinator will offer advice.

r. Medical equipment for loan. Over a period of several years, members and friends donated medical equipment items (e.g., wheelchairs, walkers, and crutches). The items are available for loan to any person in need.

s. Duet: Partners in Health & Aging. Our church partners with Duet, an interfaith nonprofit organization. Founded in 1981, Duet promotes health and well-being through services to homebound elders and adults with disabilities, caregivers, faith communities, and grandparents raising grandchildren across the Phoenix, Arizona, area. Duet's vision is a community where every person ages with compassion, dignity, and hope.

We have eleven members from our church who are active volunteers and give of their time through Duet to assist adults in need. Duet pairs compassionate volunteers with homebound "neighbors" who can no longer drive yet wish to remain living in their own homes. Free-of-charge volunteer services include grocery shopping, transportation to medical appointments, visits and phone calls, paperwork assistance, home repairs, respite, computer training, and home-safety assessments.

Duet offers the coordination needed to transform volunteers' good intentions into action. Services not only meet essential needs, but also relieve the isolation and depression common among homebound elders. Strong bonds of friendship are the norm. The average neighbor receives assistance for 2.7 years, although many "duets of service" last far longer. Duet staff members recruit, screen, train, fingerprint, supervise, insure, match, and recognize volunteers and receive requests for assistance and conduct home visit assessments. By working in partnership with Duet, our church can focus on inspiring members to serve others and referring people in need, rather than providing the coordination needed to effectively carry out this type of service. The care ministry team has a coordinator/liaison who reserves rooms at our church and hosts Duet trainings for new volunteers from time to time.

Duet helps participating congregations begin or maintain health programs. Duet offers courses that provide registered nurses the training to serve as faith community nurses. Ongoing training and support help congregational health programs flourish. Services offered through congregational health programs include health screenings, navigation and advocacy, health education, referrals, and personal-health counseling. Our church was listed in Duet's 2015 annual report as a model for offering a wide range of care ministries that build health in mind, body, and spirit.

Our congregation keeps an eye out for members who are caring for their aging loved ones. Many family members and friends do not consider such care "caregiving." They are just doing what comes naturally to them. However, that care may be required for months or years and can take an emotional, physical, and financial toll. By encouraging them to call Duet, they may tap into free-of-charge support groups, respite, workshops, book clubs, movie matinees, retreats, guidance, and referral information.

Parenting isn't easy, especially the second time around. In Maricopa County, over thirty-two thousand grandparents are solely or primarily responsible for one or more grandchildren. Our church has several grandparents in this situation. Duet provides tools, resources, and support so that these and other grandparents are prepared to care for their vulnerable grandchildren and themselves. Grand families receive help through support groups, respite, family activities, benefit counseling, workshops, legal guidance, and accurate referral information. By helping grandparents persevere under challenging conditions, children can remain in stable, loving homes rather than enter the foster care system.

Our care ministry team sponsors a special offering from our church for Duet once every two years. We help make Duet a vibrant source of help and hope through our gifts of time and dollars. Through our partnership, our members receive help in times of need, as well as the opportunity to flexibly and safely serve neighbors in our midst. Duet's website is: www.duetaz.org.

t. Cancer care ministry. When my wife received the good news that she was in remission, we decided we would like to train others to be cancer care ministers. Prior to Velma (my wife) being diagnosed with cancer, we attended the pilot training session at the Cancer Treatment Centers of America (Our Journey of Hope).

That year was a blur with doctors' appointments, chemo, and radiation. We heard from Cancer Treatment Centers of America (Our Journey of Hope) inquiring about how training was progressing for our church. I explained my wife had been through cancer treatment and was in remission. I was informed of a class being offered, and it was suggested we take the class and be commissioned. We did complete the refined training from the pilot session we attended almost two years earlier.

Within a few months, we advertised in our local church news to determine who might want to attend cancer care training. Eight individuals expressed interest, including those who had experienced cancer themselves, lost loved ones to cancer, had close friends with cancer, and others who wanted training so they could help others. Our steps we followed were the following:

✓ Set up an informal meeting for eight interested people and provided an overview of the training with time for questions. We provided coffee and cookies to spark thoughts and ideas, and all eight decided on the training.

✓ The program has eight sessions with training materials, which includes a short video for each session. We discussed with the eight and agreed each of our times together would be longer, and the eight lessons would be taught at four meetings.

✓ Each session went well with great interaction. The class members were experienced in the subject of cancer, and we also addressed the challenges of being a caregiver for a cancer patient.

✓ At the last meeting, we discussed how cancer care ministry would work in our church. We decided it would not be limited to training specifically to assist those with cancer but the team would also be available for caregivers.

✓ The members were unofficially commissioned at this last meeting by my wife and me. We were provided with the appropriate information, and our two pastors officially commissioned the graduates from the class.

✓ The class members have been assigned, and reports are provided to our coordinator.

The cancer journey we experienced has been a blessing in helping others. We've grown in discernment and faith that God is present whether we are ascending to a hilltop or walking through a valley. It took some time for us to know how to proceed after the pilot training, but God was in the whole process. We are grateful for God's healing hand and privilege to help others in need and give God the glory in all we do.

The training supplied by the Cancer Treatment Centers of America/Our Journey of Hope (CTCA/OJOH) is excellent.

4. Care ministry training:
   It was decided we would use *Christian Caregiving: A Way of Life* by Kenneth C. Haugk (copyright 1984). Mr. Haugk is the founder of Stephen Ministry Services, a system of lay caring ministry, and he is executive director of Stephen Ministries. Our instructors were the two Stephen Ministers who were helpful in the early stages of development.

5. Who and what is the care ministry team:
   The team consists of the pastors and members of the congregation who volunteer their time to visit, call, and assist those in need. The volunteers in the church are servant-leaders just as Jesus was a servant-leader. The team's responsibilities, goals, and objectives are aligned and strategically focused with engaged hearts, minds, and spirits.

6. The keys to success:
   We knew it would take prayer, Bible study, spiritual growth, ongoing training for each ministry, and teamwork to be successful. An added requirement is clear commu-

nication with other team members and our pastors. Team members must communicate between themselves and with the chair. The pastors are included in the communication process to share thoughts and approval. The methods for sharing can be through phone, e-mails, face to face meetings, etc.

7. The key benefits:

   ✓ Implementation of a response to a need can be a quick phone call, e-mail, text, etc.
   ✓ Minimal changes will be necessary when a new pastor is assigned to the congregation.
   ✓ Frequent meetings are not needed if there is ongoing and clear communication with team, chair, and pastors.
   ✓ It is cost effective since the team consists of dedicated and trained volunteers and there is no budget. Dollars for the team are raised through bake sales, shirt sales, card sales, etc., and earnings to a designated fund.
   ✓ Practice succession planning by allowing coordinators to select and train their replacement when they are ready to step down. The coordinators are aware their successor must have a passion for that ministry. John Maxwell stated in his book *Encouragement Changes Everything: Bless and Be Blessed*, "Experts spend a lot of time trying to figure out what makes people successful, and more than anything else, passion is what makes the difference."[46]

8. Role of chair:

   ✓ Be a servant-leader and change agent.
   ✓ Choose and empower passionate and dedicated coordinators.

✓ Communicate but do not micromanage.
✓ Communicate with pastors and have their support (which is critical).
✓ Apply principles of CLTE (change, leadership, teamwork, and encouragement).

You have now learned about the benefits of volunteering, the challenges of change and the basic tools of change, leadership, teamwork, and encouragement. We have also shared a care ministry model made up of volunteers with a passion for serving others.

We invite you to step into the next chapter and become a change agent where you will have an opportunity to design and create your own care ministry model.

We hope you enjoyed your journey through Caught Caring and how you too can experience the inner joy, peace, and satisfaction, along with the exciting adventures at different stages of ministry.

CHAPTER 5

Become a Change Agent and Design Your Own Care Ministry Model

Change – Leadership – Teamwork - Encouragement

"I alone cannot change the world, but I can cast a stone across the waters to create many ripples" *(Mother Teresa).*

Design Your Own Care Ministry Team Model

The purpose of this last section is for you to create and design a care ministry team model for your church or organization. The "model for serving others" described in the previous chapter is a proven model that can work in any size church or organization. Please use the nine steps listed below as well as change, leadership, teamwork, and encouragement (CLTE) in your final design.

Step 1. Create a mission statement. If you would like to create a design other than a bicycle wheel, it should be included in step 1.

_____

_____

_____

_____

Care Ministry Team Design

Step 2. Identify ministries that clearly work successfully, with or without a coordinator. If a coordinator is not in place, locate one and remember that each coordinator should have a passion for their ministry.

_____

_____

_____

_____

Step 3. Brainstorm and identify new ministries that would be beneficial.

It is important to begin on a small scale. Remember, a care ministry team is always an ongoing process. Each new ministry requires a coordinator.

_____

_____

_____

_____

Step 4. Develop or identify an existing training program to be attended by all team members. A recommendation is *Christian Caregiving - A Way of Life* by Kenneth C. Haugk (Augsburg Publishing House, copyright 1984).

_____

_____

_____

_____

Step 5. Brainstorm and develop a statement that identifies who and what your new care ministry team represents for your organization.

_____

_____

_____

_____

Step 6. Develop a statement that identifies the keys of success for the team.

_____

_____

_____

_____

Step 7. Develop a statement that identifies key benefits of your team. It is important to know the benefits in order to accomplish in helping to meet the needs of your church or organization.

_____

_____

_____

_____

Step 8. Develop the role of the team chair. Once completed, a chair should be appointed. It is possible for the chair (staff or volunteer) to be appointed early in the process.

_____

_____

_____

_____

Step 9. Implement the team, and as mentioned before, it is an ongoing ministry, and change is going to happen. If a ministry does not seem to be working, it should be discontinued, and other new ministries can be added as the care ministry continues to grow.

_____

_____

_____

_____

NOTES

1. Joel Osteen, <u>Your Best Life Now: 7 Steps to Living at Your Full Potential</u>, (New York, NY: Warner Faith, Time Warner Book Group, 2004), 221.
2. Stephen Post and Jill Neimark, <u>Why Good Things Happen to Good People</u>, (New York, NY: Broadway Books, 2007), 1.
3. William Jefferson Clinton, <u>Giving-How Each of Us Can Change the World</u>, (New York, NY: Borzoi Book, Alfred A. Knopf, 2007), 33.
4. Laura Arrillaga-Andreessen, <u>Giving 2.0; Transform Your Giving and Our World</u>, (San Francisco, CA: Jossey-Bass, 2012), 16.
5. "Volunteer Your Way to Success," The Arizona Republic, April 18, 2016, section 10A.
6. "The Health Benefits of Volunteering: A Review of Recent Research," The Corporation for National and Community Service, accessed April 2007, www.nationalservice.org.
7. Post and Neimark, <u>Why Good Things Happen to Good People</u>, 54.
8. David Dunn, <u>Try Giving Yourself Away</u>, (New York, NY: Prentice Hall, 1970),1.
9. Brad Formsma, <u>I Like Giving</u>, (Colorado Springs, CO: Waterbrook Press, 2014), 6.
10. Arrillaga-Andreessen, <u>Giving 2.0; Transform Your Giving and Our World</u>, 18.

11. Anne Graham Lotz, <u>Why? Trusting God When You Don't Understand</u>, (Nashville, TN: W. Publishing Group – Division of Thomas Nelson Publishing, 2004), 125.

12. Gretchen Thompson, <u>God Knows Caregiving Can Pull You Apart</u>–12 Ways to Keep It All Together, (Notre Dame, IN: Sorin Books, 2002), 97-99.

13. "Things I've Learned in Life," The Arizona Republic, January 11, 2016, section 10A.

14. Don Lumley, "The Ice Cream Thieves," Angels On Earth (May–June 2010) 18–22.

15. James W. Moore, <u>You Can Get Bitter or Better!</u> (Nashville, TN: Abingdon Press, 1989), 23–24.

16. Post and Neimark, <u>Why Good Things Happen to Good People</u>, 272.

17. Greg Gilpin, <u>Why We Sing</u>, (New York, NY: Shawnee Press, Inc.,2005).

18. Randy Kilgore, "You Missed the Chance," Our Daily Bread, (October 27, 2016).

19. Richard Carlson, "Make Service an Integral Part of Your Life," in <u>Don't Sweat the Small Stuff . . .</u> and It's All Small Stuff (New York, NY: Hyperion, 1997), 179.

20. Carlson, "Do Something Nice for Someone Else and Don't Tell Anyone About it," in <u>Don't Sweat the Small Stuff . . .</u> and It's All Small Stuff (New York, NY: Hyperion, 1997), 23.

21. "Volunteering A Noble Way to Receive a Varsity Letter," The Arizona Republic, July 15, 2014, section A12.

22. Formsma, <u>I Like Giving</u>, 33.

23. John Amodeo, "Intimacy, A Path Toward Spirituality 5 Reasons Why Receiving Is Harder Than Giving," Psychology Today, <u>https://www.psychologytoday.com/blog/intimacy-path-toward-spirituality/201402/5-reasonswhyreceiving isharderthangiving/PsychologyToday</u>.

24. Formsma, <u>I like Giving</u>, 163.

25. Ken Blanchard and Phil Hodges, <u>The Servant Leader: Transforming Your Heart, Head, Hands and Habits</u>, (Nashville, TN: J. Countryman, A division of Thomas Nelson, Inc., 2003), 65.

26. John P. Kotter, Leading Change, (Boston, MA: Harvard Business School Press, 1996), 65–66.
27. James W. Moore, You Can Get Bitter or Better! 9.
28. Robert Schuller, Don't Throw Away Tomorrow, (New York, NY: Harper Collins Publishers, Inc., 2005), 228–229.
29. Dennis Stevenson, "What Is a Change Agent?" Toolbox, last modified April 15, 2008, http://it.toolbox.com/blogs/original-thinking/what-is-a-change-agent-23764.
30. Tommy Spauldings, The Heart Led Leader, (New York, NY: The Crown Publishing Group, A division of Penguin Random House, LlC., 2015), 88.
31. Moore, You Can Get Bitter or Better! 11.
32. Warren Bennis and Burt Nanus, Leaders: The Strategies for Taking Charge, (New York, NY: Harper and Row Publishers, 1985), 21.
33. David B. Yoffie and Michael A. Cusumano, Strategy Rules: Five Timeless Lessons from Bill Gates, Andy Grove, and Steve Jobs, (New York, NY: Harper Collins Publishers, 2015), 18-19.
34. Kotter, Leading change, 95.
35. John C. Maxwell, Encouragement Changes Everything: Blessed and Be Blessed, (Nashville, TN: Thomas Nelson, Inc., 2008), 99.
36. Spauldings, The Heart Led Leader, 2.
37. Ibid., 58.
38. "Things I've Learned in Life," The Arizona Republic, January 11, 2016, section 10A.
39. Peter M. Senge, Art Kleiner, Charlotte Roberts, Richard B. Ross, and Bryan J. Smith, The Fifth Discipline Fieldbook: Strategies and Tools for Building a Learning Organization, (New York, NY: Doubleday Dell Publishing Group, Inc., 1994), 6.
40. Maxwell, Encouragement Changes Everything: Blessed and Be Blessed, 103.
41. Spauldings, The Heart Led Leader, 180.
42. Donald B. Egolf, Forming Storming Norming Performing: Successful Communication in Groups and Teams, (Lincoln, NE: Writers Club Press, An Imprint of: iUniverse, Inc., 2001), 102.

43. Joel Osteen, <u>Everyday A Friday – How to Be Happier 7 Days A Week</u>, (New York, NY: Faith Words Hachette Book Group, 2011), 235–236.

44. Maxwell, <u>Encouragement Changes Everything</u>, 9.

45. Spauldings, <u>The Heart Led Leader</u>, 151.

46. Maxwell, <u>Encouragement Changes Everything</u>, 116.

ABOUT THE AUTHOR

Dr. J. Don Trotter is married, lives in Glendale, AZ, has two beautiful daughters who are married to wonderful sons-in-law and there are five handsome grandsons. Don grew up in Florida, received his bachelor and master's degrees from University of South Florida and Doctorate from Nova Southeastern University. He served his country in the US Army and is proud to be an American. Don taught college in the area of marketing along with other courses related to business administration and worked in the corporate sector.

While working for a corporation, Don volunteered his own time to develop and implement a successful Market Masters Competition program that continued to be offered annually. The competition challenged undergraduate and graduate students to design a marketing plan for a chosen corporation's products or services that was then presented at the corporate headquarters. Senior executives from business units were judges and winners received gifts of products, exposure to company leaders and possible future employment. It was a win-win for the students and the corporation.

Don and his wife are active in a local church where they co-chair a care ministry team. Don enjoys playing tennis, riding his motorcycle, and traveling . He has had the opportunity to travel to Asia, Europe, South America, and many places in North America. Don and his wife enjoy keeping in touch with friends they've known in locations where they have lived. Don credits his wife for this since she sends notes, makes phone calls and tries to make personal visits. It is a blessing from God to have great friends.